AIR WAR
over
Southeast Asia

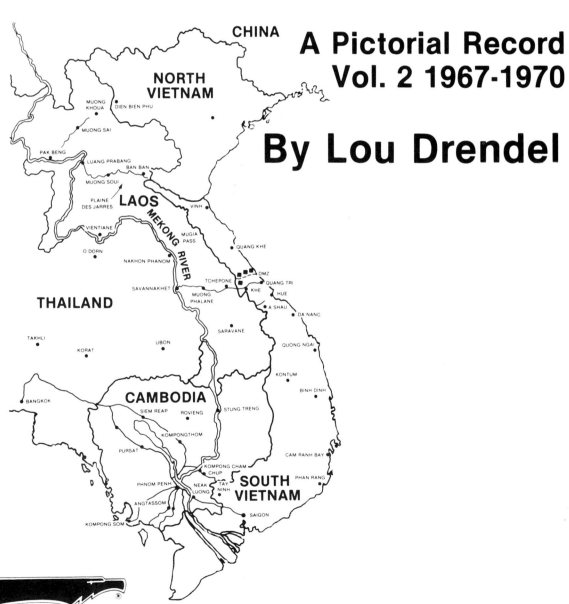

CHINA

A Pictorial Record
Vol. 2 1967-1970

By Lou Drendel

NORTH VIETNAM

MUONG KHOUA
DIEN BIEN PHU
MUONG SAI
PAK BENG
LUANG PRABANG
BAN BAN
MUONG SOUI
PLAINE DES JARRES
LAOS
VINH
VIENTIANE
MUGIA PASS
O DORN
MEKONG RIVER
NAKHON PHANOM
QUANG KHE
TCHEPONE
DMZ
QUANG TRI
SAVANNAKHET
KHE
HUE
THAILAND
MUONG PHALANE
A SHAU
DA NANG
TAKHLI
SARAVANE
KORAT
UBON
QUONG NGAI
KONTUM
BINH DINH
BANGKOK
CAMBODIA
SIEM REAP
ROVIENG
STUNG TRENG
KOMPONGTHOM
PURSAT
CAM RANH BAY
KOMPONG CHAM
CHUP
PHAN RANG
PHNOM PENH
NEAK LUONG
TAY NINH
SOUTH VIETNAM
ANGTASSOM
SAIGON
KOMPONG SOM

squadron/signal publications

COPYRIGHT © 1983
SQUADRON/SIGNAL PUBLICATIONS, INC.
1115 CROWLEY DRIVE, CARROLLTON, TEXAS 75011-5010

ISBN 0-89747-140-7

If you have any photographs of the aircraft, armor, soldiers or ships of any nation, particularly wartime snapshots, why not share them with us and help make Squadron/Signal's books all the more interesting and complete in the future. Any photograph sent to us will be copied and the original returned. The donor will be fully credited for any photos used. Please send them to: Squadron/Signal Publications, Inc., 1115 Crowley Dr., Carrollton, TX 75011-5010.

Photo Credits

USAF
U.S. Navy
U.S. Army
U.S. Marine Corps
Norman E. Taylor
Norm Malayney

F.C. Brown
Andy Mutzig
Jim Hurley
Al Piccirillo
Dave Evans

Brigadier General Robin Olds commanded the 8th TFW during 1967, and became the leading MiG killer with four victories.

(Back Cover) A North Vietnamese MiG 17 pulling into firing position behind an F-4. They were often able to do this even without the aid of GCI, because of the Phantom's very visible exhaust, which earned it the nickname "Smoker".

Air War Over Southeast Asia 1967

By the beginning of 1967 the danger of a communist military victory in South Vietnam had been averted. The introduction of American ground combat troops, and the resulting aggressive pursuit of Viet Cong and North Vietnamese Regulars, had turned the tide of the war in the favor of the allies. The communists had suffered heavy losses whenever they were engaged in combat with allied units, which were supported by overwhelming firepower in the form of artillery and air support. The strategic aerial power, capable of destroying the war-making potential of the North Vietnamese at it's source, was in place. There was every reason to feel optimistic about the future of South Vietnam, whose dynamic young Prime Minister, Nguyen Cao Ky, had brought political stability and reform to it's government. All that was needed to bring the war to a satisfactory conclusion was the political wisdom and fortitude to press all of these advantages, or so it seemed in 1967.

Unfortunately, the Johnson Administration could not seem to produce anything but political equivocations. Bombing halts and peace initiatives continued to emanate from Washington, while Hanoi steadfastly clung to their basic negotiating position, which was: "Stop the bombing, get out of Vietnam, then we'll negotiate." That, of course, meant that Hanoi would continue from where they had been stopped by American intervention. And without the final, conclusive, military moves necessary to convince Hanoi that they could not only not win, but could suffer defeat and the loss of what they had already gained in the North, there was little doubt in the minds of most pragmatists that the war would become a very long war of attrition.

A war of attrition against a guerrilla army, which has been provided the luxury of sacrosanct sanctuaries to which they can retire to lick their wounds and prepare to fight another day, is a war no army could hope to win. LBJ should have heeded the words of another famous American. General George

**For of all sad words of tongue or pen,
The saddest are, "it might have been".**
John Greenleaf Whittier: Maud Muller

Patton had affirmed that; "Americans will not tolerate a loser." And *not winning* was *losing* in the minds of many Americans. The Johnson Administration now had the United States involved in an undeclared war that it was apparently not prepared to take beyond a stalemate. In order to buy approval, albeit tacit, of his Vietnam policies, LBJ decided to forego the call up of reserves; even as American strength in Southeast Asia passed 400,000 men. There was no call to sacrifice through additional taxes, no rationing, and no propagandizing of Ho Chi Minh as an Asian Hitler (though his surrogates would later prove themselves as adept at genocide as Hitler's minions had been). Had any of the above steps been taken in conjunction with the military moves that had been taken, the American electorate might have demanded a declaration of war and a quick end to it. Instead, the American people were expected to acquiesce to LBJ's call for "a great deal of patience" in dealing with the war. But there were enough victories throughout 1967 to appease public opinion.

Operation Bolo

1967 started auspiciously, as the USAF scored a major victory over the North Vietnamese Mig interceptor force. Throughout 1966 the Migs had built-up their confidence and competence, becoming a major deterrent to American bombers. The Migs were tightly controlled from the ground through the use of radar. In this way, the controllers were able to position their interceptors behind the bombers, then clear them for firing runs on the American aircraft. Even when they didn't shoot the bombers down, they quite often were successful in forcing them to jettison their bombs before getting to the target. Since the major Mig bases at Gia Lam, Kep, Phuc Yen, Cat

Nakhon Phanom AB, Thailand, from which much of the clandestine aerial operations of the Vietnam War took place. (USAF photo by SSgt R. Wickley)

Phan Rang AB, RVN, home of the 35th TFW, which flew F-100s, as it appeared in December, 1970. (Norman E. Taylor)

Nha Trang AB, RVN, home of the 2nd Air Division, VNAF. They used it for a training base. 1970 photo by Norman E. Taylor.

Bi, and Kien An were off-limits to the bombers, (political equivocation) the Migs had only to land when the situation was not to their liking. Seventh Air Force Headquarters hit upon the idea of drawing the Migs into a battle with F-4 Phantoms, equipped for the air superiority mission, but masquerading as F-105s loaded for an interdiction mission.

Dubbed **Operation Bolo,** it was commanded by one of the best combat leaders in the Air Force. If the Vietnam War had enjoyed the popular support of World War II, then Robin Olds would undoubtedly have become one of it's folk heroes. An All-American football player at West Point in the 1940's Olds graduated in time to fly 107 combat missions over Europe, becoming a quadruple ace in the process. After the war he co-founded the USAF's first jet aerobatic team, and in conjunction with an exchange program, became the first foreigner to command the RAF's famous Number One Squadron, flying the RAF's first operational jet fighter, the Meteor. He married Ella Raines, one of the most beautiful and glamorous of Hollywood stars. He was a man's man...a fearless combat commander whose concern for his men earned him their everlasting respect and loyalty.

Colonel Robin Olds had arrived at Ubon, Royal Thailand Air Base (RTAB) on September 30, 1966, to take command of the 8th Tactical Fighter Wing. The 8th was known as the ''Wolfpack'', and under Olds' leadership, would become the top scoring air-to-air combat unit in the pre-bombing halt air war. In his 1967 Christmas Tour of Southeast Asia, Bob Hope dubbed it ''the largest distributor of Mig parts in the world''. With credentials like these, it was no wonder that Seventh Air Force picked the 8th to spearhead Bolo. Other units that were involved included the 355th, 388th, and 366th Fighter Wings.

If the North Vietnamese had suspected that a force of fighters was coming north for the specific purpose of destroying as many of their interceptors as possible, they would have simply remained on the ground. In order to get them up, it was necessary to disguise the forces as another of the, by now, regular flights of F-105 bombers. The two fighter forces, divided into west and east groups, (the 8th was west, the 366th east) used F-105 tanker tracks, altitudes, frequencies, airspeeds, and call signs to convince the North Vietnamese radar operators that they were a force of bombers. They were also equipped with ECM pods for the first time. The pods were programmed to jam NVA SAM and AAA acquistion, and tracking radars.

The F-105s of the 355th and 388th Wings would fly regular ''Iron Hand'' missions. ''Iron Hand'' was the name given SAM suppression flights of F-105s, which were directed by two seat F-105Fs equipped with Radar Homing and Warning (RHAW) sets which enabled them to pinpoint the location of Fansong radar sites and to warn of impending SAM firings.

The force was comprised of 14 flights of four F-4Cs, six flights of F-105s, four flights of F-104s, and EB-66s, RC-121s and, of course, the KC-135 tankers. It is important to remember that at this time U.S. fighter pilots had received very little training in air-to-air combat. As a consequence, the briefings for this mission took the better part of three days and included specific tactics to combat the Migs as well as the general mission numbers.

Bad weather delayed takeoff for an hour on the big day...January 2, 1967. All other flying had been cancelled in order to ensure that all resources were concentrated on this mission. This also gave the first flight into the target area, led by Olds, the luxury of firing at any targets they acquired, without visual or IFF identification, since they could be presumed to be enemy aircraft.

When the word to go finally came through, the Phantoms took off in flights of four, spaced five minutes apart. They had planned to arrive in the target area with that spacing, which would allow for any delayed reaction from the Migs, and ensure at least an hour's worth of Phantom coverage in the target area. As it turned out, only the first three flights of Phantoms encountered Migs. The entire target area was covered by a low, flat cloud deck. True to form, the Migs stayed low while their controllers tried to vector them into position behind the Phantoms. When they did pop through the undercast, they were immediately attacked by the F-4s. The final tally for Bolo was seven Mig-21s destroyed for no Phantom losses.

Within a week two more Mig-21s fell to pilots of the 8th, who ''disguised'' themselves by flying patterns and routes normally associated with reconnaissance aircraft, drawing the attention of four Mig-21s.

These losses seemed to take the heart out of the North Vietnamese, who stood down for additional training for the next several weeks. The effect on the American press was dramatic. Stories ap-

Colonel Robin Olds, commander of the 8th TFW, and leader of Operation Bolo. (USAF)

Colonel Daniel ''Chappie'' James, Vice Commander of the 8th TFW during Olds' tenure. His black panther was the antithesis of the Black Panthers who became such media stars in the United States during the Vietnam War. (USAF)

Olds taxies in after his last mission as CO of the 8th. He is in his personal aircraft, which bears the name that all his fighters carried in every war in which he flew. This "Scat" is number XXVII. Two of his four Vietnam victories were scored in this aircraft.

Members of Olds' flight help to get the traditional final mission party going.

(Above) F-4C of the 25th TFS "Assam Dragons". This aircraft was the personal mount of the 25th CO, Lt. Col. Lloyd Uhlrich, who named it "Miss Magic". The 25th was one of the Ubon-based 8th TFW. September, 1968 photo by Al Piccirillo.

(Below) The Phantoms of the 25th TFS on the tanker inbound to targets in southern North Vietnam. The 25th began their combat tour in May, 1968 and flew most of their missions into lower North Vietnam until a full bombing halt in November put North Vietnam off limits. Their missions were flown to other parts of SEA from November 1. August, 1968 photo by Al Piccirillo.

5

(Above) "Ol Eagle Eye" was F-4D 66-7764 of the 435th TFS, 8th TFW at Ubon in November, 1968. An F-4 of the 8th TFW flew the last strike mission of the "Rolling Thunder" campaign on 31 October, 1968. (Al Piccirillo via Norm Taylor)

(Below) One of the techniques used for bombing over familiar terrain was "Sky Spot", in which radar offsets were used to determine bomb aiming points. This enabled the bombers to drop from high altitude, through solid overcast, as in this August, 1968 mission in which 8th Phantoms dropped from 32,000 feet. (Al Piccirillo via Norm Taylor)

Major Al Piccirillo and Lt Ted Brom of the 25th TFS prior to a mission against North Vietnam, 1968. (via Norm Taylor)

(Below) F-4D of the 433rd TFS "Satan's Angels", 8th TFW at Ubon, October, 1969. The major components of the 2,000lb PAVEWAY laser guided "smart bomb" are displayed in front of the aircraft. (USAF photo by A1C Calvin O. Cruce)

peared in the major media comparing the Phantom pilots with the knights of the air of World War I. Morale was high among American pilots, and it appeared that there really was a light at the end of the tunnel.

One of the saddest aspects of the air war over Southeast Asia, particularly in the high threat areas, was the manner in which it's execution affected those who were called upon, day after day, to risk their lives. There were several periods of the war in which almost open mutiny among the troops occurred. Not just among the enlisted "grunts", whose most infamous reaction to an ambitious or stupid commander who put them in what they considered unnecessary jeopardy was "fragging" (assasination most often accomplished by rolling a grenade into the subject's tent or foxhole). The pilots who mutinied most often did so by either ignoring targeting restrictions, or by going public with their frustrations over the ridiculous rules of engagement set down by politicians, and agreed to by senior commanders.

In a pair of devastatingly bitter, *and accurate,* appraisals of the policies that were being followed in Southeast Asia, an "anonymous" USAF pilot and a retired Navy pilot, both fighter pilots, wrote to Aviation Week & Space Technology magazine during the fall of 1966, detailing their frustrations with: The bomb shortage which had emphatically and repeatedly been denied by Secretary of Defense McNamara, but which in fact did exist. In order to disguise the shortage, both the Navy and the Air Force flew their aircraft with a fraction of their load-carrying capability. This in order to build up the number of sorties flown. Whether or not this ploy was ordered by Washington is a moot point. The fact is, someone in the chain of command thought that numbers were more important than results. That spoke volumes concerning our resolve to actually win the war, both to the enemy, and to those who were actually doing the fighting. The literal license taken in describing what was actually destroyed. "VC Structures, Boats, or Irrigation Plants" were likely to actually be grass shacks, dugout canoes, and crude water wheels. Risking multi-million dollar airplanes and highly trained aircrew in an attempt to destroy such questionable targets just didn't make much sense to the pilots. The gradual erosion of motivation caused by these policies eventually led to a "safety first" policy. Many commanders, feeling they could not justify the risk involved in destroying such inconsequential targets, simply raised bombing altitudes and instituted restrictions designed to protect the crews. The net result was even less effect for the effort expended.

When a mission such as Bolo came along, even though it was inspired by the very restrictions that the pilots so detested, it generated a boost in morale out of proportion to its real strategic importance. (The purpose of air superiority is to make sure that your bombers are unimpeded in their efforts by enemy fighters. What good does it do to shoot down the enemy fighters when the bombers are not allowed to strike the most important targets in the first place?) When it succeeded beyond the wildest expectations, morale went sky-high. For once, the pilots had been able to accomplish everything they set out to, without worrying about targeting restrictions. But, as one of the letter writers correctly pointed out: *The North Vietnamese will never make peace while they are in a position to win, and when you are carrying the battle to the enemy, fighting on his ground, you are the one presently ahead.* All of the ground fighting to that time had been done on "our" ground — in South Vietnam.

Other mutinous reactions to official policy, vis-a-vis the air war, included the career-destroying protection of two of his pilots by a Wing Commander. The pilots had shot back at ships in the harbor at Haiphong, and were threatened with courts martial for this act of self-defense. The Wing Commander simply destroyed the incriminating gun camera films. On an even higher level, a very senior theatre commander carried out his own air war against an enemy who was at the time protected by one of the numerous bombing halts. A far more common reaction was simply to get out when the opportunity presented itself. The services lost thousands of highly skilled professional pilots to civilian air carriers simply because of the level of frustration in fighting to maintain the status quo ante.

The military kept constant pressure on the White House to relax its restrictive rules of engagement, and there was enough movement in this direction to keep most senior commanders appeased. General William Westmoreland, commander of the Military Assistance Command Vietnam (MACV) insisted on being given authority to authorize strikes against North Vietnam and Laos when the involved targets presented an imminent threat to the troops he commanded.

"Betty Lou" was flown by Col. A.K. MacDonald, C.O. of the 388th TFW, the first F-4E wing in Southeast Asia. Photo was taken at Ubon while the 388th was TDY due to runway repairs at their home base of Korat RTAB. January, 1969. (Al Piccirillo via Norm Taylor)

One of the most popular weapons for low level air to ground work was the high drag "Snakeye" bomb. Fins popped open upon release, retarding the fall of the bomb, enabling the "bomber" to avoid the same fate as the "bombee". (USAF)

In many cases, by the time strategic targets in North Vietnam were released for strikes, their worth had diminished. Such was the case of the POL storage facilities around Hanoi and Haiphong, whose destruction in 1966 made world-wide headlines. Unfortunately, by the time they were hit, most of the critical supplies of POL had been dispersed to the countryside, stored in containers as small as 55 gallon drums.

Since the Johnson Administration was unwilling to destroy enemy war material while it was in the relatively vulnerable marshalling areas of North Vietnam, the military was forced to hit it while in the pipeline enroute to...or worse still...after it had arrived in South Vietnam and was being used to kill allied troops. The majority of this material and manpower came down what came to be known as the Ho Chi Minh Trail, a series of snaking roads and trails that wound their way through Laos and Cambodia. The Laotion government placed restrictions on targets it would allow U.S. pilots to hit, though it was unable to stem the tide of North Vietnamese invaders itself. Nothing resembling a dwelling could be hit, even if it quite obviously sheltered an anti-aircraft weapon. No target could be hit if it was more than 206 feet off one of the trails. It didn't take the communists long to start pacing off 207 feet before they emplaced their AAA. Then, to add insult to the very real danger of injury, U.S. pilots were not given credit for missions flown over Laos, since we did not "Officially" acknowledge these missions.

At the beginning of 1967 U.S. aircraft losses in Southeast Asia had climbed to 854, including 463 over North Vietnam, (459 fixed wing and 4 helicopters.) and 391 over South Vietnam. (140 fixed wing and 251 helicopters.) While the Johnson Administration was not willing to call up the Reserves or Air National Guard, the air war did have an effect on these two units. Scheduled replacement of older National Guard equipment was postponed so that equipment losses could be replaced in the regular Air Force units in Southeast Asia. Since the production lines had long since closed down on many of the major combatant aricraft, (notably the F-100 and F-105) there was no way to make good on these losses without transferring equipment from unit to unit, or assigning different aircraft types to operational units.

Another form of attrition began to manifest itself at this time. In addition to the defections from the ranks of professional military personnel because of dissatisfaction with the conduct of the war, there was the policy of rotation out of the combat zone after you had finished a specified tour. In order to replenish the ranks of experienced combat pilots, it was necessary to cross train pilots of other types of aircraft. Thus, it was not unusual for a C-130 pilot to find himself in the cockpit of an F-4, dodging flak over Hanoi. Or for a B-52 pilot to be plucked from his 40,000 plus foot perch to fly a 100 knot

The first F-4Es to join the 388th did not carry the Sharkmouth, which was added later. 301 is loaded with Mk 82 500lb "slick" (low drag) bombs and CBUs. (USAF)

(Above) F-4Es of the 388th TFW formate on the tanker, pre-strike, 1970. The Phantom in the background carries the name "Paper Tiger". (USAF photo by SSgt John A. Evans)

knot FAC aircraft at a few hundred feet over the triple canopy jungles. The Air Force cross trained pilots. The Navy did not. In the Navy, if you were a fighter pilot, you were a fighter pilot for life. (There were subdivisions of that category within the Navy, to be sure. "Interceptor" pilots were looked down on by the clear air mass dogfighting fighter pilots.) And if you were an Attack "Puke", that is what you remained throughout your operational carrier. That did not change the fact that the Navy combat pilots were just as frustrated with the rules of engagement as their Air Force brethren, but it was a much smaller community, and the facts of life concerning carrier aviation may have served to dilute some of the natural resentment felt by pilots. Physiological studies done during the war showed that pulse and respiratory rates might be higher during a carrier recovery than during the bomb run. When you subject yourself to the high risk environment of the flight deck, on a day-to-day basis, peacetime or war, you are liable to have a slightly different view of risk-taking in operational flying. The lure of the most challenging operational flying in the world...off and on carriers...kept the Navy supplied with pilots despite any frustrations they may have felt with the strategy of U.S. politicians.

During a 1968 visit to the carrier Kitty Hawk, while it was tuning up off the Southern California coast, prior to a deployment to WestPac, I heard a young A-7 pilot exclaim; "Hell, I wish they would let us go North again! (the bombing halt was in effect) You can't win any medals bombing South Vietnam!" The upwardly mobile career officer realized that there were certain squares that had to be filled, and though no one was thinking about losing the Vietnam War at that point, if they had thought about it, they would certainly have come to the conclusion that an act of bravery that won them the medal would not be diminished by the outcome of the war. Erosion of morale did not set in until the consequences of political folly were seen on a first person basis.

F-4E of the 34th TFS, 388th TFW. (USAF)

"Little Chris" of the 388th loaded with a pair of ECM pods, but no external weaponry. (USAF)

RF-4C of the 11th TRS, 432nd TRW taxies in after a 1969 mission from Udorn RTAB. Under the 1968 bombing halt agreement, reconnaissance flights were allowed to continue over North Vietnam. The North Vietnamese had agreed not to fire upon them, but like most of their agreements, they broke it repeatedly, which led to armed escorts who were allowed to shoot back. (USAF)

During the bombing halt of 1968-72 Thailand-based USAF fighter bombers flew most of their missions in support of troops in South Vietnam, or against targets along the Ho Chi Minh Trail in Laos. (USAF)

In spite of the fact that their conventional war was not going so well in South Vietnam, the North Vietnamese continued to infiltrate guerrillas into Laos and Thailand, using Russian supplied helicopters operating out of North Vietnam and China, and French Sud-Alouette helicopters flown from Cambodia. The USAF worried that the communists might stage a major assault on one of it's bases in Thailand. Of particular concern were the bases at Nakhon Phanom and Udorn, the two closest to Laos. By this time the Laotion Government controlled no more than a third of it's country, with the communists in firm control of at least half of Laos. U.S. airpower alone prevented a total communist takeover of Laos. It also served to keep the communists from mounting any major attempt to capture or destroy Udorn or Nakhon Phanom.

The North Vietnamese' Russian and Chinese allies were beginning to step up their shipments of war material into North Vietnam. Soviet ships were visting Haiphong on an average of 10 per month, and the only satisfaction in that for the allies was that the growing rift in Sino-Soviet relations had made sea shipments necessary. (Whenever the Russians shipped overland, through China, the Chinese would paint out the Russian markings on supplies, replacing them with Chinese markings.) The nine Mig-21s which were shot down in the first week of January had been replaced by the first week of February. Automatic Anti-Aircraft weaponry was sprouting from the North Vietnamese countryside like steel asparagus, and the number of prepared Surface-to-Air Missiles (SAM) sites increased daily. The SAMs had not been as devastingly effective as some of their publicity might have indicated. Of the 470 U.S. aircraft shot down over the north through 1966, only 30 had been bagged by the SAMs. But they were effective in forcing strike aircraft to lower altitudes, where the AAA was deadly. In fact, the SAMs were somewhat cumbersome and difficult to manage. Their size and the distinctive shape of the sites made them targets that were hard to miss. As a consequence, the North Vietnamese often kept the missiles concealed in anticipation of a large raid, and as the Wild Weasels increased in effectiveness, SAMs waited for a good shot before firing. It was estimated that there were up to 1000 anti-aircraft weapons in North Vietnam at this time, with most of them being radar directed. Electronic Countermeasures (ECM) was becoming an increasingly vital adjunct to every strike force, with most strike aircraft carrying some kind of their own individual radar jamming capability, and the entire force being escorted by ECM aircraft such as the EB-66. A greater percentage of each strike force was devoted to anti-personnel weaponry targeted for SAM and AAA sites.

In South Vietnam, the principle communist anti-aircraft weaponry continued to be of the 30 caliber variety, with a few instances of 50 caliber or 37MM fire being reported. This was attributed to the fact that interdiction of the Ho Chi Minh trail was preventing movement of the heavier anti-aircraft weapons into the South.

Air operations in South Vietnam consisted of a wide variety of missions, flown by dozens of different types of aircraft. The first American parachute assault of the war took place on 22 February 1967, during **Operation Junction City,** when the 2nd Battalion of the 503 Infantry, 173rd Airborne Brigade jumped into the infamous War Zone C, a long-time Vietcong stronghold north of Tay Ninh City. Operation Junction City also employed the 1st and 25th Infantry Divisions, the 11th Armored Cavalry Regiment, the 196th Light Infantry Brigade, and parts of the 4th and 9th Infantry. Twenty-one C-130s were used to deliver the 780 combat troops of the battalion and their heavy equipment. This freed up the helicopters needed to deliver other units to the combat zone. The 11th, 145th, and 1st Aviation Battalions flew 9,700 sorties, lifting 9,518 troops and an average of 50 tons of cargo per day during Junction City, which lasted until the middle of May and accounted for 2,728 known enemy casualties. Large caches of medical supplies and rice were captured. War Zone C, which had been a virtually impregnable VC stronghold since the days of French occupation, was no longer a haven for the Viet Cong.

Junction City was not the only large scale operation conducted by ground forces early in 1967. There was no less than ten major combat operations begun or continued during the first two months of 1967. These accounted for the staggering total of 16,565 known enemy casualties! These were offensive operations...the well known ''search and destroy'' missions.

In spite of these successes in taking the offensive against the communists, and against the advice of the military, from the Pentagon to the on-scene commanders, Secretary McNamara still favored establishment of a defensive line to try to stop infiltration. He envisioned a fence, stretching across the

F-105 of the 354th TFS, 355th TFW loaded with Mk 84 2,000lb bombs and Mk 82 500lb bombs, all with fuse extenders to ensure that they explode before burying themselves in the ground. (USAF)

Ground crewmen of the 457th TFS load a strike camera aboard a Thud prior to a 1970 mission. It is loaded with M117 750lb GP bombs, favored for hard targets, such as heavily fortified bunkers. (USAF)

F-105F of the 354th TFS acts as background to armament specialists preparing 750lb bombs for loading. (Fairchild Republic)

DMZ and through Laos, which would be made up of electronic sensors that could warn of enemy activity and pinpoint it's location. Several electronic sensors were developed and air-dropped over the Ho Chi Minh Trail, and they did help to pinpoint activity on the trail. But locating targets was not the problem. There were targets aplenty in North Vietnam. Getting permission to strike those targets was the problem. (Of 81,000 sorties flown against the North in 1966, only 1% had been against the 94 target list drawn up by JCS in 1964.)

"The Polish Glider" was flown by Major Don Kutyna with the 44th TFS, 355th TFW. The name was in reference to the gliding properties of the Thud, which rivaled those of a brick. The inscription under the Polish Flag declares that the pilot is a "Yankee Air Polack", a correction of the oft-stated North Vietnamese alliteration to American pilots as "Yankee Air Pirates". (B/G Don Kutyna)

There were many in the Johnson Administration who were convinced that: (A) We should not be in Vietnam in the first place and (B) That if their boss insisted upon being there, they would do everything in their power to sabotage the efforts of the military to win the war. To that end, they produced studies which proclaimed that airpower could not prevent North Vietnamese aggression in the South; then lobbied hard to emasculate the military's efforts to use airpower effectively. In his October, 1966 report to President Johnson, Secretary McNamara had recommended that we: "Stabilize the Rolling Thunder program against the North at the current monthly level of 12,000 sorties because to bomb the North sufficiently to make a radical impact upon Hanoi's political, economic and social structure, would require an effort which we could make but which would not be stomached either by our own people or by world opinion; and it would involve a serious risk of drawing us into open war with China." In lieu of winning the war, he suggested that we "Take steps to increase the credibility of our peace gestures in the minds of the enemy through both political and

(Above) "Fat Fanny" was an F-105F of the 33rd TFS, 355th TFW. It flew in the Wild Weasel role. The Wild Weasel 105s carried Shrike radar homing missiles, and Standard ARM missiles, both designed to home on radar emmissions of enemy AAA and SAM sites. In the early stages of Rolling Thunder, the F-100F was employed in the Wild Weasel role, with accompanying F-105s carrying the ordnance to attack the sites once they were located by the 100s. The F-105s were known as "Iron Hand". The F-105F Wild Weasel replaced the 100F during the fall of 1966. Large strikes normally employed one flight of 4 F-105F Wild Weasels to keep the enemy down.

(Below) Armorers check the M-61 20MM Vulcan cannon on an F-105F prior to a 1967 Rolling Thunder mission against North Vietnam. (USAF)

military moves." He suggested that we consider a decision to stop all bombing of North Vietnam, or alternatively, to shift the weight of effort away from Zones 6A and 6B (Hanoi-Haiphong) and concentrate the war instead on the infiltration routes in Zones 1 and 2. He also suggested trying to create a rift between the Viet Cong and North Vietnam by making room for them in the government of South Vietnam. It may not have been out and out surrender, but McNamara's recommendations were the next thing to it. Naturally, the military resisted these suggestions mightily.

In a report submitted to the Secretary concurrently with the McNamara report, the JCS stated: "The Joint Chiefs of Staff do not concur in your recommendation that there should be no increase in level of bombing effort and no modification in areas and targets subject to air attack. They believe our air campaign against NVN to be an intergral and indispensable part of over all war effort. To be effective, the air campaign should be conducted with only those minimum constraints necessary to avoid indiscriminate killing of population." Prophetically, they went on to say; "The Joint Chiefs of Staff believe that the war has reached a stage at which decisions taken over the next sixty days can determine the outcome of the war, and, consequently, can affect the overall security interests of the United States for years to come."

The JCS showed their impatience with the public and the tentative manner in which the war was being fought as their memo continued; "The frequent, broadly-based public offers made by the President to settle the war by peaceful means on a generous basis, which would take from NVN nothing it now has, have been admirable. Certainly, no one — American or foreigner — except those who are determined not to be convinced, can doubt the sincerity, the generousity, the altruism of U.S. actions and objectives. In the opinion of the Joint Chiefs of Staff the time has come when further overt actions and offers on our part are not only nonproductive, they are counterproductive. A logical case can be made that the American people, our Allies, and our enemies alike are increasingly uncertain as to our resolution to pursue the war to a successful conclusion."

The last sentence of the foregoing paragraph provided the most insightful analysis of what continuing the policy of gradual escalation would achieve. Unfortunately, the collective opinion of the Joint Chiefs was given less weight than that of the Presidents civilian advisors when it came to the probable reaction of the communists to continued equivocation in the use of our military power.

In contrast to the basically pessimistic report submitted by McNamara in late 1966, Special Assistant to the President Robert W. Komer had this to say after a February 1967 visit to South Vietnam. "Wastefully, expensively, but nonetheless indisputably, we are winning the war in the South. Few of our programs — civil or military — are very efficient but we are grinding the

enemy down by sheer weight and mass. And the cumulative impact of all we have set in motion is beginning to tell." That was just what LBJ wanted to hear, for it reinforced his decision to continue to wage the war on the political cheap. No additional taxes...no call up of the Reserves or National Guard...and no slackening in his costly and futile war on poverty at home. Guns and Butter would continue to be the official policy from Washington, thus sowing the seeds of alternating periods of inflation and recession, which would become more frequent throughout the 70's and result in near bankruptcy in the 80s.

General Westmoreland, eager to capitalize on the successes of 1966, requested additional troops, with a projected in-country force strength of 555,741 men by mid-1968. In a March 18, 1967 memo, he made the following comments concerning the American role, past and future:

> ...our operations were primarily holding actions characterized by border surveillance, reconnaissance to locate enemy forces, and spoiling attacks to disrupt the enemy offensive. As a result of our buildup and successes, we were able to plan and initiate a general offensive. We now have gained the tactical initiative, and are conducting continous small and occasional large-scale offensive operations to decimate the enemy forces; to destroy enemy base areas and disrupt his infrastructure; to interdict his land and water LOC's and to convince him, through the vigor of our offensive and accompanying psychological operations, that he faces inevitable defeat.

Westmoreland realized that if the current policy of containing the war on the ground to the south were maintained, then it would not be enough to just kick the NVA out of the south. The U.S. would have to provide South Vietnam with the wherewithal to protect itself from further subversion, internal or external. His memo continued;"Military success alone will not achieve the U.S. objectives in Vietnam. Political, economic and psychological victory is equally important, and support of Revolutionary Development (RD) program is mandatory. The basic precept for the role of the military support of Revolutionary Development is to provide a secure environment for the population so that the civil aspects of RD can progress." But he seemed to be intent upon acheiving military victory when he submitted additional troop requests for fiscal year 1968, which would bring U.S. strength to 678,248. Under this plan, American forces would engage and destroy the enemy while the South Vietnamese forces pursued the Revolutionary Development programs designed to win the hearts and minds of the peasants, whose first loyalty has always been to their families.

It was a plan which would prove nearly impossible to implement. Militarily, it was an unqualified succcess. American troops continued their hot pursuit of the NVA and VC, scoring victory after victory. There was simply no question of American superiority in every meaningful category of tactical warfare. American mobility, firepower, and individual skill clearly outclassed the communists. Strategically, the enemy was a formidable foe, made the more so by a hostile American Press, whose collective opposition to the war turned many of them into stooges of the North Vietnamese.

Though the Americans understood well the priority of loyalty practiced by the peasantry...that is, from bottom to top (family first, then hamlet, province, and very vaguely, country), and hoped to increase the loyalty felt to the central government of the South through the RD programs, the methods sometimes used were counter-productive. Since it was impossible to occupy every hamlet, day and night, quite often the guerrillas would return when American or South Vietnamese troops left. Very often brutal revenge was taken on villagers who cooperated, actively or passively, with the Allies. The villagers were squarely in the middle. In the areas where the enemy was most active, a program of relocation was instituted. The villages were evacuated and the areas designated as "Free Fire Zones". Anything or anybody within that area was considered enemy, and was dealt with accordingly. The results were a tactical victory, but a strategic disaster. For, by removing the villagers from their cherished land, the land venerated as home and final resting place of their ancestors, the Allies were not making friends of the people in whose name the war was being fought. It was additional fall-out from the political decision taken in the United States to contain the ground war to the South.

The desire of the Johnson Administration to fight the war on the sly...to get it over with as quickly as possible, with as little inconvenience as possible, encouraged the massive use of American manpower and firepower. Our South Vietnamese allies were simply overwhelmed by this, and left in the backwash of the logistical tidal wave that swept their country as the American buildup reached it's zenith.

Though he hoped to end the war quickly, there is ample evidence to indicate that President Johnson was repeatedly warned that continuing the policy of gradual escalation would lengthen the war. In a meeting with Generals Westmoreland and Wheeler in April, 1967 Johnson was told that Allied forces were now destroying enemy forces more quickly than they could be replaced. Estimates of the time needed to win the war range from 2 to 5 years, depending upon how many additional troops were sent to Vietnam. At this time, there were 470,000 troops authorized, with as many as an additional 200,000 on request. The JCS was pressing for more concerted action, including possible attacks against North Vietnamese bases in Laos, Cambodia, and in North Vietnam itself. The President asked what would happen if no more American troops were added to the fight. General Wheeler's reply was that, while we wouldn't lose the war, the enemy might regain some of the initiative, and the war would undoubtedly drag on for years longer.

In May, 1967 Johnson received a memo from one of his principale advisors, McGeorge Bundy. In his memo, Bundy acknowledged the probability that the military would seek additional troops and authorization to bomb more significant targets in North Vietnam. He recommended that Johnson turn these requests down. His reasons for rejecting strategic bombing of the North were rooted in his rejection of it's effectiveness (later proven to be totally inaccurate, when the all-out Lineback II campaign caused a North Vietnamese cave-in within two weeks), and in the fear of political ramifications in the United States.

Bundy was opposed to the troop increases on the basis of the political price that might have to be paid for their introduction. He had one eye on the 1968 election, and with the accepted "no-win" policy of the Administration, there seemed little choice other than to try to keep the lid on the seething political cauldron of Vietnam. The risks of winning the war still seemed more dangerous to Washington than the price of preventing the communists from winning. There was a feeling that the American electorate would tolerate a holding action, but would not pay the price of a victory. Over the next two

The Cessna O-2A replaced the O-1 Birddog as the standard USAF FAC (Forward Air Controller) aircraft. The military version of the 337 Skymaster carried rocket pods for target marking, and additional windows in the right door to aid the FAC in spotting targets. The aircraft at top is taxiing out at Bien Hoa AB in October, 1969. It belonged to the 19th Tactical Air Support Squadron (TASS). The aircraft below was assigned to Detachment 1, 504th Tactical Air Support Group (TASG), a unit which provided academic and flying indoctrination for new FACs at Phan Rang AB. (USAF)

years, that assessment would prove to be 180 degrees from reality.

Regarding future options in the air war over North Vietnam, Presidential assistant for national security Walt W. Rostow outlined his opinions in a report to Secretary of State Dean Rusk the same month. As Rostow saw it, we had the choice of (A) going all out against the North, destroying not only their ability to make war, but also their ability to import war-making material. (B) Continuing to destroy what they had already imported, with restrictions on where it could be attacked, or (C) abandoning the attacks on the northern, most heavily defended portions of North Vietnam in favor of hitting the lower portions and the infiltration routes more heavily. He made clear his feeling that whatever we did, the Soviet Union was not likely to risk an all-out confrontation over Vietnam, nor would China come in unless we invaded the northern areas of North Vietnam. In spite of this, he too, opted for political equivocation, recommending that we continue with option B, since he believed that we were hurting the North Vietnamese, and if we kept at it long enough they would get the message sooner or later that we were not going to quit.

McNamara made clear his view that it would certainly be later, asserting in a May 19, 1967 report to the President that; "With respect to interdiction of men and material, it now appears that no combination of actions against the North short of destruction of the regime or occupation of North Vietnamese territory will physically reduce the flow of men and material below the relatively small amount needed by enemy forces to continue the war in the South." In this same report he acknowledged the North Vietnamese' ability and indeed their intent to absorb punishment at the current level. He recommended following a course similar to (C) above. The most significant thing in this report though, is his reasoning for this slackening of effort.

In McNamara's opinion, "There may be a limit beyond which many Americans and much of the world will not permit the United States to go. The picture of the world's greatest super power killing or seriously wounding 1,000 non-combatants a week, while trying to pound a tiny backward nation into submission on an issue whose merits are hotly disputed, is not a pretty one. It could conceivably produce a costly distortion in the American national consciousness and in the world image of the United States — especially if the damage to North Vietnam is complete enough to be "successful".

McNamara's description of North Vietnam as a "tiny backward nation" is a good indication of the kind of thinking that led to the ineffective policies of the Johnson Administration. That "tiny backward nation" had the 4th largest army in the world by 1975, and was demonstrably the most aggressive, muderous national presence in Asia. Where he got his figure of 1,000 non-combatants a week is not specified, nor is his assertion that the issue in question had hotly contested merits. The issue was the invasion of South Vietnam by North Vietnam. The people contesting the merits of our defense of South Vietnam were our enemies, and some of our more addle-brained public officials. Throughout the war, survey after survey showed that the majority of Americans were in favor of our stated objectives in the war. Most Americans felt that we were not doing enough to win the war, and would have been appalled at the idea of the rest of the world dictating American policy in fighting aggression.

The rift between the Joint Chiefs and their civilian boss was widened as McNamara's view of what could be accomplished militarily continued to diverge from theirs. In an August, 1967 appearance before the Senate Armed Services Preparedness Investigating Subcommittee, USAF Chief of Staff General John P. McConnell defended the interdiction campaign against North Vietnam as successful and necessary. He reported that the bombing campaign had forced the North Vietnamese to employ over 500,000 full and part time workers in lines of communication repair and air defense. He quoted figures that showed how the bombing had, in effect ruined the economy of the North, and forced the communists to go from an exporter (Prior to 1964, 1.7 million tons exported, 1 million tons imported) to an importer of over 4 million tons per year. In spite of the massive buildup of the air defense system. U.S. losses had dropped from 3.2 per 1000 sorties in 1965 to significantly less with twice the sorties flown during 1967. He pointed out that the campaign against North Vietnam was the only offensive action where the initiative was firmly in our contol. Without the aerial campaign, the enemy would be free to send many thousand more troops into the South, and our casualties would be much higher. He asserted that: "Airpower, in affording this advantage exerts the influence that is most likely to force the enemy to reconsider his avowed hard line."

In his year end report to the JCS, Admiral U.S. Grant Sharp, CINCPAC, noted that: *From 1 January, 1967 to 15 December, 1967, 122,960 attack sorties were flown in Rolling Thunder route packages I through V and in Laos. SEA Dragon offensive operations involved 1,384 ship-days on station and contributed materially in reducing enemy seaborne infiltration. Air attacks throughout North Vietnam and Laos destroyed or damaged 5,261 motor vehicles, 2,475 railroad rolling stock, and 11,425 watercraft from 1 January through 20 December, 1967.* In spite of this impressive tally, he admitted that enemy transportation capability was largely unchanged from the end of 1966, due to replacement of these items by the Russians and Chinese communists. Most of the replacement materials were entering North Vietnam through it's principal port, Haiphong. To no avail the JCS continued to urge that the North Vietnamese be denied the use of Haiphong through mining, and/or attack of the port facilities. And in a typical example of inverse reasoning, opponents of the war pointed to the failure of airpower to deny war material to the communists as reason enough to maintain Haiphong's exempt status on the target list.

UH-1F Gunship of the 14th Air Commando Squadron, 20th SOS. The "Hornets" operated in III Corps area of South Vietnam in 1967. This USAF Huey is armed with the 7.62MM 6,000 rounds-per-minute minigun. (USAF)

Rescue and Recovery

From the humble beginnings of just three officers and three enlisted men at Tan Son Nhut AB in 1962, the rescue forces of USAF grew to impressive proportions at the height of Rolling Thunder operations. This first detachment had no aircraft of it's own and had to rely on U.S. Army and Marine Corps crews to accomplish the rescue mission. The first USAF helicopters assigned for the specific purpose of rescue and recovery were the HH-43s of units in the Philippines and Okinawa. The first unit formed with it's own aircraft arrived at Nakhon Phanom in June, 1964. They had two HH-43s and 36 personnel. They were augmented by HU-16 Albatrosses from the 31st ARS at Clark AFB, PI, which deployed two of the Grumman amphibians to Danang to aid in making rescues from the Gulf of Tonkin. Later that year three modified HH-43F helicopters arrived at Bien Hoa. They were equipped with armor plating and 250 foot cables to penetrate the heavy triple canopy rain forest. By the time the first Rolling Thunder strikes were flown, there were five helicopter detachments assigned to USAF rescue within the war zone. They were at Bien Hoa, Danang, Udorn, Nakhon Phanom, Takhli, and Korat. The units at Udorn and Nakhon Phanom were specifically tasked with recovery of downed aircrew.

The first H-3 helicopters used by rescue forces were a pair of CH-3s on loan from TAC in the summer of 1965. The first HH-3Es specifically outfitted for search and rescue arrived that fall. In the meantime, control of rescue forces had passed from HU-16s to SC-54s to the HC-130 version of the Hercules, which became the definitive SAR command and control aircraft. The A-1 Skyraider had emerged as the most effective escort to rescue helicopters, since it's relatively slow speed most closely matched that of the helicopters it escorted. It had the range and load-carrying capabilities to provide protective cover to downed aircrew while the rescue missions were carried out. During the course of these missions, the A-1 also racked up the highest loss ratio of any airplane in Southeast Asia, with a loss rate per 1,000 sorties of up to 6.2 over North Vietnam.

At the beginning of 1967, there were 50 Aerospace Rescue and Recovery Squadron (ARRS) rescue aircraft in Southeast Asia. These were five HU-16Bs at Danang, nineteen HU-43Bs, and ten HH-43Fs used for local airbase rescue, ten HH-3Es for operations into Laos and North Vietnam, and six HC-130s for control of rescue operations. One of the most significant pro-

HH-3E of Detachment 1, 40th Aerospace Rescue and Recovery Squadron, Nakhon Phanom AB, Thailand preparing for takeoff on a February, 1969 rescue mission. The HH-3 was the original "Jolly Green Giant".

A pararescue specialist (PJ) looks for downed aircrew from the doorway of a 40th ARRS HH-3. (USAF)

(Above) An early HH-3 prepares for takeoff from Udorn. Later models were equipped with aerial refuelling capability, which gave them the range necessary to fly missions deep into North Vietnam. (USAF)

(Top) F-100 pilot, Capt Bernard E. Flanagan of the 355th TFS relaxes in the HH-3E of the 3rd ARRG which picked him up after his 25 February, 1968 shoot down in South Vietnam. He was picked up within an hour. (USAF)

(Above Left) Sandy (A-1 Skyraider) and Jolly Green (HH-53B) crew pose prior to a mission from Udorn AB, Thailand. (USAF)

(Left) Another satisfied customer, 1Lt Gordon K. Breault arrives at Nakhon Phanom after his rescue in February, 1969. Rescues are recorded as parachutes behind the cockpit window. (USAF)

(Below) HH-3E of the 40th ARRS at Nakhon Phanom AB in February, 1969. (USAF)

The HH-43 provided the only dedicated rescue capability early in the war and helped to develop many of the techniques which were later perfected by the HH-3 and HH-53. This HH-43F was assigned to Phu Cat AB in January, 1968. (USAF via Norm E. Taylor)

blems faced by ARRS in Southeast Asia was the distances involved in attempting to rescue downed aircrew in the more heavily defended areas of North Vietnam. The rescue helicopters were range limited, and were forced to use forward ground refuelling bases in Laos. These "Lima Sites" were often insecure, suffering shelling by the Pathet Lao and facing the constant threat of being overrun. In addition to this, the political consequences of being caught in "neutral" Laos caused more than a little consternation in command circles.

The accepted wisdom was that helicopter aerial refuelling was impossible with state of the art technology. Fortunately, a few innovative thinkers in the H-3 Systems Project Office at Wright Patterson AFB disagreed with conventional thought. Mr. Richard Wright, Mr. James Eastman, and Major Harry Dunn thought they could prove aerial refuelling was possible. Dunn attached a refuelling probe to the front of an H-3, talked the Marines into letting him attempt a rendezvous with one of their KC-130s, and proved that you could in fact refuel a helicopter from a C-130. The Air Force was quick to modify it's HH-3s and C-130s, and the first operational refuelling took place in Southeast Asia on June 21, 1967. The first HH-53B Super Jolly Green Giant helicopters arrived in September, 1967. They had twice the gross weight of the HH-3E, with over four times the useful load. They were able to hover at higher altitudes, which made rescue from the mountains of North Vietnam more certain. They also had more defensive armament than their predecessors. The three 7.62MM miniguns gave the HH-53 fearsome firepower. By the end of 1970, the 3rd Aerospace Rescue and Recovery Group had made over 2,000 saves.

The HH-43 Huskie used the call sign "Pedro" and came to be known as such throughout SEA. It was used extensively to provide air base fire suppression and rescue. It is shown with the fire-fighting package used to contain air base fires. (USAF)

(Left) The HH-53B "Super Jolly Green Giant" had the power and range to perform all rescue and recovery missions and was even used in the recovery of downed aircraft, in this case an Air America Huey that lost an engine over the Central Highlands of South Vietnam, July, 1968. (USAF)

(Bottom) One of the more unusual aircraft employed in the war was the YQU-22A Pave Eagle, which was used in the Igloo White anti-infiltration program along the Ho Chi Minh Trail. Nakhon Phanom AB, January, 1969. (USAF)

1968

None but yourself who are your greatest foe

Emerson

If 1967 had started with auspicious victories, the following year was just the opposite. Anti-war feeling in the United States had reached fever pitch. The Administrtion's failure to demand sacrifice from the American people, and to portray the North Vietnamese as the vile tyrannical government that it was, had led to a war-weariness among the traditional supporters of the American government during time of crisis. The middle classes saw themselves as the victims of the war. Their sons were doing the fighting and dying. Their taxes were paying for the war, while the Great Society programs of the Johnson Administration encouraged indolence among those it was supposed to help. Those who still supported the war were frustrated with the weak and ineffectual manner in which the administration was directing the military effort.

The United States Government was walking a tightrope. It's slow, painful approach to fighting the war was wearing the enemy down, but it was also wearing down the political support needed to continue the war. If the war had continued to develop as it had in 1966 and 1967, that support might have remained. But the communists once again sacrificed tactical victory for strategic advantage.

In July of 1967 the North Vietnamese decided to launch a general offensive throughout South Vietnam. Within a month the South Vietnamese got wind of this offensive and began warning the Americans. In a September radio broadcast the North Vietnamese Defense Minister, Vo Nguyen Giap, warned that there would be stepped up fighting in the near future. In November U.S. forces in Quang Tin captured documents ordering a general offensive, with attacks on the lowlands and a takeover of Saigon. In a December speech, General Earle Wheeler, chairman of the JCS, warned that, while we were winning the war, it was quite possible that the enemy would attempt one last ditch offensive, similar to the Battle of the Bulge in World War II. And that same month General Westmoreland warned Washington that the communists had decided on intensified attacks in an effort to win the war. President Johnson warned Australian Prime Minister Holt that "Kamikaze" attacks were coming in Vietnam.

A-1E loaded with rocket pods and bombs for a 1968 rescue escort mission from Udorn RTAB. Though it had the range and ordnance carrying capability, the relatively slow speed of the Skyraider made it a tempting target for NVA gunners. "Sandy" (the call sign of A-1 rescue escorts) pilots often flew into the teeth of the defenses to protect downed aircrew, and as a consequence, suffered the highest loss rate of any airplane in SEA. (USAF photo by MSgt Manuel A. Collaso)

On-Mark modified B-26Ks flew "Nimrod" interdiction missions against the Ho Chi Minh Trail from Nakhon Phanom. (USAF)

A-1H of the 22nd SOS, 56 SOW after it was lifted off the runway at Ubon, after a forced, wheels-up landing. Sandies often limped back to bases in Thailand shot-up from battles in North Vietnam. (Al Piccirillo via Norman E. Taylor)

On 5 January 1968, a U.S. Press Release in Saigon reported the communist order to flood the lowlands and attack Saigon and other cities, calling for a general uprising of people against the Saigon Government. On 15 January Westmoreland predicted that these attacks would come either just before or just after the Tet holidays.

On 21 January the first concentrated attacks on the Marine base at Khe Sanh occured. This was the beginning of a siege which would capture so much national attention, and whose result would cause so much controversy. Two days later the North Koreans captured the U.S. intelligence ship Pueblo. Johnson's response to this was to call up 14,787 Reservists and to send the nuclear carrier USS Enterprise to Korean waters. The Pueblo had been steaming in international waters, and it's capture was a blatant act of piracy. The North Koreans refused to return the ship or it's crew, and treated the reserve call-up and the approach of the Enterprise with disdain. It was a prescursor of events to come, as totalitarian states began getting the message that the United States lacked the will to use it's power in a decisive manner.

On 30 January at 12:35 AM the first attacks of what came to be known as the Tet Offensive took place. Nha Trang, as well as two cities in I Corps and five cities in II Corps were struck. The allies cancelled the Tet cease fire, which had been called the day before, in celebration of the traditional Vietnamese new year. Unfortunately, many of the South Vietnamese Army units had already released much of their strength to go on leave during the holiday. The following night the dam burst and the all out communist offensive which had been predicted began. Virtually every major city in South Vietnam was struck, including Saigon. The result was momentary chaos. A nineteen member sapper team even breeched the wall of the U.S. Embassy in Saigon and remained on the premises until the following day, when they were rooted out and killed by embassy guards.

These dramatic attacks, futile though they were, galvanized the American press. The television networks reported that the heaviest fighting of the Vietnam War was going on, and that the U.S. and Vietnamese casualties were heavy. The only city in South Vietnam that the communists managed to capture and hold for any length of time was the old Imperial City of Hue. Within two days President Johnson was calling the Tet Offensive a complete failure militarily. In support of this, MACV announced casualty figures of 12,704 communists killed, with 318 U.S. and 661 South Vietnamese deaths in the same time period. President Thieu of South Vietnam called for stepped up bombing of North Vietnam in retaliation for the Tet attacks.

Though the fighting continued throughout that spring, for all intents and purposes, the military result was in by the end of February, when General Wheeler sent a memo to President Johnson detailing the Tet scoreboard. He said: "Enemy losses have been heavy; he has failed to achieve his prime objectives of mass uprisings and capture of a large number of the capital cities and towns. The South Vietnamese Army held up against the initial assault with gratifying, and in a way, surprising strength and fortitude. They were

The venerable Cessna O-1 Birddog was still used as late as 1970. "Ronnie's Racer" belonged to the 21st TASS at Phu Cat AB. (Norman E. Taylor)

The OV-10A became the fastest, most heavily armed of the pure FAC airplanes. It was developed originally as a COIN (Counter-Insurgency) aircraft. It carried four 7.62MM machine guns in its sponsons and was able to carry small bombs as well as rocket pods used to mark targets. (USAF)

The F-100 Super Sabre continued to carry the brunt of the "in-country" air war through 1968. This aircraft belonged to the Colorado Air National Guard, which had been called to active duty in 1968. The Hun below was from the 416th TFS at Phu Cat AB. (USAF)

not badly hurt physically-they should recover strength and equipment rather quickly. Their problems are more psychological than physical. U.S. forces have lost none of their pre-Tet capability."

The final cost to the communists, as reported in former Prime Minister Nguyen Cao Ky's book on the war, was 34,000 killed. American estimates were higher, up to 40,000 killed, with 3,000 captured and 5,000 disabled. It was a stunning defeat for the communists. The Viet Cong was virtually wiped out as a political cadre. From this point on, there could be no doubt about who was doing the bulk of the fighting, or who would benefit from a communist victory. The North Vietnamese no longer had to worry about the charade of an indigenous communist movement within South Vietnam. A communist victory would produce one Vietnam...run from Hanoi.

Though that might have been clear at the time, the American press prefer-red to concentrate on the negative aspects of Tet. Instead of hailing the great military victory that Tet proved to be for the allies, they reported that the military had tried to deceive the American public about progress toward the end of the war. It was an election year, and political opponents of LBJ were not about to point out that he had been scrupulously honest about progress. The press had become openly hostile, and during a news conference, Secretary of State Rusk asked the rhetorical question; "Whose side are you on?" Walter Cronkite, with all the military expertise and acumen amassed in a lifetime of being a reporter, declared the war a stalemate. He was promptly invited to Hanoi. NBC commentator Frank McGee declared that the United States was losing the war. On March 31, the President announced a partial cessation of bombing of North Vietnam, and his withdrawal from the Presidential Election Campaign.

The Seige of Khe Sanh

The Khe Sanh combat base straddled Route 9 in northwestern South Vietnam. It was 16 kilometers from Laos and 25 kilometers from the DMZ. It was within easy striking distance of large numbers of North Vietnamese troops, who could be expected to take Route 9 in any large scale drive to the coast. American intelligence had seen the coming onslaught of the Tet Offensive, and Khe Sanh was reinforced accordingly. U.S. Army Special Forces had occupied Khe Sanh from 1962 until 1966, when a Marine battalion dug in on its plateau. Navy Seabees lengthened and improved the 1500 foot dirt runway. It's 3,900 feet were now enough to accommodate aircraft up to and including the C-130.

The Marines actively patrolled the area around Khe Sanh and, during one such patrol in April, 1967, they discovered North Vietnamese bunkers on hill 861 which seemed to indicate that the NVA intended to attack Khe Sanh. The Marines reaction to this was to insert more troops and begin more active patrols. Several bloody battles ensued, which resulted in the enemy being knocked off hills 881N, 881S, and 861. These were three of seven major peaks overlooking the base from the north.

The whole idea of establishing a major combat base in some of the toughest terrain in Southeast Asia, where it would be a constant source of trouble to North Vietnamese troops using the Ho Chi Minh Trail or attempting to mount a major offensive in I Corps was like throwing down the gauntlet. American commanders were sure that the North Vietnamese would react. The Americans reasoned that Giap would see a parallel between Khe Sanh and Dien Bien Phu, and would mount a major attempt at overrunning the base. Like the French at Dien Bien Phu, the Americans wanted to have a chance to destroy large numbers of North Vietnamese troops in a major bat-

tle. Unlike the French, the Americans had the weaponry to do the job.

The siege of Khe Sanh started with a barrage of mortar and artillery directed at the base on January 21, 1968. One of the enemy shells hit the base ammunition dump, which blew up destroying 98% of the ammunition on the base. They also managed to crater 1,500 feet of runway badly enough to prevent its use. In spite of this, USAF C-123s managed to keep the base supplied while heavy air strikes around the base the following day caused dozens of secondary explosions and fires. It had become obvious that the North Vietnamese had risen to the bait and now had the base surrounded with thousands of troops.

With the combat base surrounded, the only method of resupply was through the air. Flying into Khe Sanh became one of the most dangerous and demanding flying jobs in the world. Because the base was surrounded by enemy troops, there were no safe approaches. Aircraft landing at Khe Sanh were subjected to a hail of 30 and 50 calibre machine gun fire. And because the base itself was on top of a mountain where the air was cool, yet humid, and sometimes trapped by the surrounding higher terrain, low clouds and fog were a constant fact of life. A major percentage of all approaches were instrument approaches, some even made at night under the uncertain light of flares. And once on the ground, the resupply aircraft became what the Marines described as "Mortar Magnets". The enemy had pretty well registered most spots on the base, and tried hard to destroy as many of the resupply airplanes as they could while they were unloading and/or loading. Unloading cargo along the taxiway, while moving, became a standard tactic.

On February 7, the North Vietnamese attacked and overan the Special Forces Camp at Lang Vei, some six kilometers west of Khe Sanh. This attack was notable for it's use of Russian built PT-76 light tanks, the first use of armor by the communists. Though the 24 defenders put up a fierce, night-long fight, and managed to destroy several of the enemy tanks with 106MM

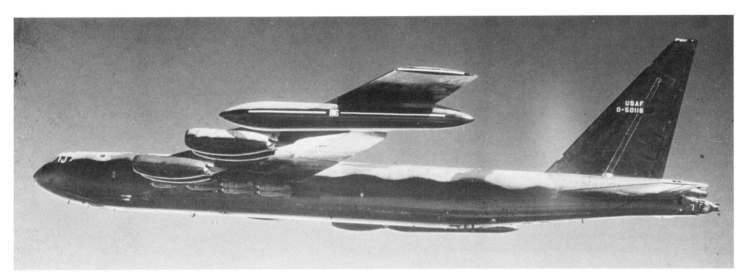

(Above) B-52 enroute to a target in South Vietnam, 22 November, 1967. The BUFs were used time after time to defeat large-scale North Vietnamese attacks, such as the September, 1967 threat to Con Thien, the Marine base south of the DMZ; or the November, 1967 battles at Dak To and Loc Ninh. Their most notable effort in this time period was the relief of the seige of Khe Sanh, in which three Marine Regiments and one South Vietnam Ranger battalion were surrounded by 30,000 North Vietnamese intent upon overrunning the combat base. B-52s provided the bulk of the bombing missions, as airpower defeated the communists.

In the photo at left, bombs are loaded aboard a B-52 at Utapao AB, Thailand in April, 1967. Operations from Utapao began that month, and added to the effectiveness of the B-52s, since most targets in the war zone were over twice as close to Utapao as they were to Anderson AFB on Guam, which had been the B-52s only base until that time. One of the significant operations flown by B-52s which did not get publicised at the time, was Operation Menu, in which B-52s flew 16,527 sorties, dropping 383,851 tons of bombs on communist sanctuaries in Cambodia, from 1969 to 1973. (USAF)

Bitter social commentary is evident in this F-100F named "PRO-TESTER'S PROTECTOR", about to taxi for a mission from Phu Cat AB in April, 1969. (USAF)

One of six F-111As sent to Takhli RTAB in 1968, for a premature combat trial, sits in the foreground as equipment belonging to the detachment is loaded on a C-141 for return to Nellis AFB, Nevada. This trial was a disaster for the public image of the 111, as three of the six aircraft were lost under circumstances that all but prevented analyzation of what had caused the losses. (USAF)

recoilless rifles and LAWs, they were finally driven from the camp after suffering 10 KIA. they retreated to Khe Sanh with the aid of a relief force.

February was the toughest month of the siege. On the 23rd of that month, over 1,300 enemy shells fell on the base. Days of 1,000 shells were not uncommon, and on occasion ammunition or fuel dumps were hit with spectacular results. The North Vietnamese continued to probe at the defenses of Khe Sanh, and to construct trenches and bunker complexes within sight of the perimeter in preparation for a major assault on the base. But, even though the weather remained at it's monsoon worst, tactical resupply via C-130, C-123, and C-7 aircraft continued. And tactical air support, using tactical fighters of the Marines and Air Force provided pinpoint destruction of any enemy units observed. B-52 Arc Light strikes provided the really heavy concentrations of aerial destruction which collapsed enemy bunkers and tunnel complexes and kept the North Vietnamese in a constant state of flux. As the weather around Khe Sanh improved, it became obvious that the long expected all-out attack on the base was not coming. The NVA continued to pump shells into the base, and Marine patrols around the perimeter occasionally ran into enemy positions, but airpower was keeping the enemy so off balance that a major attack seemed impossible to mount.

General Westmoreland had dubbed the aerial bombardment of enemy positions surrounding Khe Sanh "Operation Niagra" because, as he said, he envisioned the falling bombs as being equal in intensity to the falls. He wasn't far wrong. Seventh Air Force flew 9,691 sorties, dropping 14,223 tons of bombs. The B-52s of 3rd Air Division flew 2,548 sorties and dropped 59,542 tons of bombs, while the Marines flew 7,078 sorties and the Navy flew 5,337 sorties, dropping 17,015 and 7,941 tons of bombs respectively. B-52s dropped bombs closer to friendly lines than at any other time previously, using the accurate and reliable sky spot system. The landscape around Khe Sanh came to resemble the moon, with crater upon crater from all the bombs and shells directed at North Vietnamese troops. Estimated enemy casualties were some 10,000 troops. Fully half of his original attacking force! American casualties at Khe Sanh were 199 KIA, 1,600 WIA. President Johnson awarded the Presidential Unit Citation to the 26th Marines, who had withstood the siege and emerged victorious.

Two North Vietnamese divisions had been decimated by the battle for Khe Sanh. It was one of the most lopsided military defeats in the history of warfare and undoubtedly took a lot of the steam out of the Tet attacks on I Corps cities. And yet, the American press described the defense of Khe Sanh as "ill-advised" at best, and "product of Presidential stubborness" at worst. This, of course, before the results were in...after the battle, the hindsight of a majority of the major media became strangely clouded. They insisted upon viewing Tet as the turning point of the war...in the enemy's favor. Enemy losses were horrifying. North Vietnam lost 30 percent of it's top ranking junior officers, and their overall casualties for 1967 and 1968 amounted to a half a million men! That, in equivalent terms, would have been the same as the United States losing 5 Million men!

North Vietnam, in the spring of 1968, was poised on the brink of defeat. Their losses, from combat and desertion, would take at least two years of respite from fighting to make up. But Lyndon Johnson's Democrat Party was also poised on the brink of defeat. His withdrawal from the Presidential race of 1968 was advertised as a "statesman-like act, designed to win the peace", it was more likely an effort to give the Democrat nominee a chance to disclaim the war policies of the Administration. Johnson had given up any hope of winning the election, and the war. The former may have been beyond his grasp in the spring of 1968. The latter was not.

The President's bombing moratorium on the north extended northward from the 20th parallel. But when the Navy launched a major attack on Thanh Hoa, a large and important North Vietnamese communication and transshipment point below the 20th, the anti-war lobby cried foul. The President, already on the run, moved the bomb-halt line south to the 19th parallel. The North Vietnamese had gained a significant strategic advantage without giving an inch in their so-called "negotiating position".

Militarily, North Vietnam was in deep trouble. Politically, they were way ahead of the game. When asked for an assesment of the situation by the JCS, Admiral U.S. Grant Sharp, CINCPAC, replied:

> As a result of the tremendous personnel losses inflicted on the enemy when he chose to come out in the open during the TET Offensive, followed by the successful offensive operations launched by the Vietnamese and Free World Forces, we now have a stronger position on the ground in South Vietnam than before the Tet Offensive. The enemy is hurting badly, both from our earlier bombing campaign in North Vietnam and from our successful operations in South Vietnam. In the near term we are militarily in a strong position — the relative balance of strength in the longer term will depend on the action taken by both sides during the negotiating period.

> The position of strength we currently enjoy could not have been achieved without the air and naval campaign against northern North Vietnam. The enemy has responded to our unilaterial limitation on these campaigns by increasing significantly his infiltration efforts and by stepping up his activities in South Vietnam. Hanoi's reaction to the current bombing limitation gives further credence to the view that the enemy will take every possible advantage of any restrictions which are imposed upon U.S./Free World military operations. If we accede further to Hanoi's demands without exacting comparable concessions, a deterioation in the overall U.S./Free World military situation in South Vietnam could develop in a gradual but steadily accelerating way. In the end we could lose at the conference table what the enemy could not take on the battlefield.

Admiral Sharp went on to warn that the enemy would not negotiate in good faith without the stimulus of continuing attacks upon his most vital facilities in the north. He warned that a continuation of the bombing restrictions would eventually lose the advantage so hard won during Tet. There is

B-57E Camberra of the 8th Tactical Bomb Squadron, 35th TFW, on the ramp at Ubon RTAB, 1969. Home base for the unit in Vietnam was Phan Rang AB. This aircraft had recovered at Ubon after losing it's right elevator and most of the stabilizer to AAA over Laos. (Al Piccirillo via Norm Taylor)

B-57E loaded and ready for a mission from Phan Rang, March, 1969. The Canberras of the 8th and 13th Bomb Squadrons ended their long tour of duty in Southeast Asia in September, 1969. Only 32 of the original 96 B-57s to deploy, survived. (USAF)

The Lockheed C-140 was used for intra-theatre VIP transport. Korat RTAB, 1970. (USAF)

RC-135 refuelling over Southeast Asia, January, 1967. (USAF)

C-133B of the 60th Military Airlift Wing, Travis AFB, California at Phu Cat AB, December 11, 1970. Utilization of the C-133 was limited by its speed, and by flight safety considerations as it neared obsolscence. (Norman E. Taylor)

(Below) C-7B "Santa Bou" Caribou of the 537th TAS departs Phu Cat AB at 0900 hours, 25 December, 1970, to deliver Christmas gifts to Vietnamese children. Markings appropriate to the occasion were applied consisting of a Red nose (radome), Flesh face, White and Red cap, with lettering for the occasion either Red outlined in White, or White outlined in Red. This became a tradition for the 527th and was one of the demonstrations of American kindness that went largely unremarked upon by the news media. (Norman E. Taylor)

"Lone Star State", a C-7B of the 457th TAS, 483rd TAW taxies past unidentifiable aircraft wreckage at Katum, during resupply operations in support of the Cambodian Incursion, May, 1970. (USAF)

(Above Left) "Suzzy Q", a C-7B of the 459 TAS, 483rd TAW, out of Cam Ranh Bay off loading supplies at Tra Bong, February, 1970.

When delivering supplies to Special Forces Camps, which were likely to be located in some of the hottest spots in South Vietnam, engines were kept running, and the supplies were kicked out the back without delay. Tra Bong, February, 1970. The Caribou was originally purchased by the Army to support its Airmobile Divisions and six companies of C-7s were sent to Vietnam. They were transferred to USAF in January, 1967, but remained under operational control of the Army. (USAF)

no evidence to believe that the Administration was in agreement with this assessment. There is ample evidence that Admiral Sharp's assessment was absolutely correct!

If the Administration was unwilling to listen to the voices of experience, the Republican Party was not. They commissioned a task force in the spring of 1968 to make an assessment of the situation in Southeast Asia. This group consisted of two former Defense Secretaries, two former Assistant Secretaries, two former chiefs of the JCS, several other four star retired military men and three members of Congress. They concluded the obvious. The McNamara policy of gradualism had encouraged a wider war, with more inherent danger of escalation into a major power conflict. It had also called into question the will of the United States in resolving armed conflicts quickly and with whatever force was necessary to ensure that our allies were victorious. They recommended that our national policy should reaffirm that we would take whatever action we deemed necessary to defeat an aggressor, and that it would not be limited by "graduated response". This was just so much whistling in the wind as far as the Johnson Administration was concerned, and by the time the new Republican Administration came to power in early 1969, any popular mandate for winning, or even continuing the war had been lost.

The so-called peace negotiations that got under way in Paris in May of 1968 were little more than a sham. They were a way for the Johnson Administration to excuse it's continued weak and ineffectual strategies in fighting the war. And they were a way for the North Vietnamese to rebuild their military machine in preparation for an all-out assault on the South, with guaranteed impunity from American bombing of their most important staging points. The North Vietnamese took advantage of this period recklessly. They moved 85,000 troops into South Vietnam, and the Ho Chi Minh Trail became one of the busiest highways in the world as thousands of tons of supplies flooded into the South. There was scant attention paid to concealing this activity, for the communists knew that the Johnson Administration was powerless to stop them. Lyndon Johnson, the politician, was now more interested in winning an election for his party than he was in winning a war for his country.

Clark Clifford, McNamara's successor as Secretary of Defense, called a meeting in Saigon in July, 1968, to assess the current situation in the war zone. In a report prepared for this meeting, Admiral Sharp warned that the enemy had regained the initiative as a result of the respite from bombing of his homeland, and that he would not negotiate seriously unless given a reason to do so. In the final, prophetic paragraph of his report, he said:

while appreciative of the need for restraint in the light of the current negotiations, recognition should also be taken of the need for timely decisions directed toward conclusion of the war by military means. Accordingly, I recommend that the air campaign against North Vietnam be resumed. Those restrictions which limit the bombing to the area south of 20 degress should be removed. This decision is time-sensitive if the advantage of the prevailing good weather are to be maximized. Postponement of a decision will prevent initiation of a concerted air and naval campaign against North Vietnam until spring of 1969. It will then require us to engage an enemy whose defenses have been reconstitued, whose resolve to continue the war will be strengthened, and whose war-making potential will have been substantially enhanced through Soviet and Chicom military and technical assistance. The consequences of such an engagement will surely be measured in higher casualties, greater costs, and potentially more dangerous risks of widening the conflict.

In a message to the JCS on the day before his retirement from active naval service on 1 August, 1968, Admiral Sharp reiterated that we possessed the forces to resume the bombing north of the 20th parallel, and that it would be necessary to do so, particularly in the Hanoi/Haiphong area, if we hoped to get the war over with quickly. His successor, Admiral John S. McCain, was in complete accord.

The U.S. negotiators at the Paris Peace Talks were Averill Harriman and Cyrus Vance, and their accomplishments from July through November, 1968 were exactly zero. For four months they sat across from the North Vietnamese, listening to a stream of invective against the American involvement in Southeast Asia. Finally, so they said, they "sensed" an understanding that meaningful talks would ensue if the United States ceased all bombing of North Vietnam.

The President's announcement of a complete bombing halt over North Vietnam came just five days before the American presidential elections. Cynics thought that it was timed to accrue maximum advantage to the Democratic candidate. It didn't. The American electorate was evidently fed up with the democrats, and Richard Nixon was elected President. Nixon's strategy for ending the war was to end American involvement, whether or not the war ended. We would still be committed to an independent South Vietnam, but they would have to do their own fighting, while we provided the logistical support to sustain them in that fight.

Minnesota Air Guard C-97 on the ramp at Tuy Hoa AB, RVN, August, 1970. (USAF photo by A1C Gary S. DePinto)

EC-121 over South Vietnam, November, 1967. The EC-121s provided the majority of airborne command and control missions during Rolling Thunder, under the call sign "College Eye". (USAF)

C-124 Globemaster running up engines prior to departure from Thailand. The 124 provided some Strategic Airlift, though its 95 hours of flying time round trip from Travis AFB, California to Saigon worked out to 13 days in mid-sixties utilization rates, and precluded its use on a large scale. (USAF)

C-123K Ranch Hand defoliation aircraft at Nha Trang AB, January, 1969. Ranch Hand Operations began in 1962, and were conducted by USAF aircraft and crews under the control of VNAF in order to preclude communist charges of U.S. chemical warfare. (USAF)

Though it had been declared obsolete in 1956, the C-123 Provider became one of the mainstays of tactical airlift in the Vietnam War. It was modified with a pair of J-85 jet engines which increased its payload carrying capability by nearly one third. The first of these modified 123s arrived at Tan Son Nhut on April 25, 1967. (USAF)

In the meantime, the bombing halt remained in effect. It's only apparent effect was to allow the North Vietnamese to repair their supply lines, reinforce their anti-aircraft defenses, and to harden worthwile strategic targets.

As he began his presidency, Richard Nixon's view of Vietnam was that it was a transitory problem, and that American foreign policy should not be limited in it's approach to other problems or possibilities by the Vietnam War. It was the new Secretary of Defense, Melvin Laird, who coined the phrase "Vietnamization" as description for turning over responsibility for the war to the South Vietnamese. President Nixon also held the belief that, as allies, the North Vietnamese were likely to become more of a thorn in the sides of the Russians or Chinese. The North Vietnamese had played one against the other as the Sino-Soviet rift widened. Nixon's view of the war and its affect on international relations was totally pragmatic and would lead to our most effective use of power during the Vietnam War...but not until the stage had been set.

(Left) AC-119G Shadow Gunship over the coast of South Vietnam, July, 1970. The C-119 Flying Boxcar was developed into a gunship as a result of the need for a more effective gunship than the AC-47, and a shortage of C-130s for this purpose. AC-119Gs carried four 7.62MM miniguns, flare launchers, Xenon light, Night Observation Sight, and a fire control computer. The first AC-119Gs arrived in Vietnam during November, 1968. (USAF)

(Below) A 15,000lb B-82 bomb is loaded on a C-130 "bomber" at Cam Ranh Bay in March, 1970. Ten and Fifteen thousand pound bombs were developed for the B-36 bomber and put into storage when the B-36s were retired. They were brought out of storage and used to blast landing zones. Some were delivered by C-130s, and some were delivered by CH-54 helicopters. A drogue chute was used to stablize and retard the fall of the bomb, which proved to be remarkably effective in blasting holes in the heavy triple canopy rain forest, even when 250 foot trees were the targets. (USAF)

Very early in his presidency, Nixon decided that the only way to achieve a military victory was through a "knockout blow", which he felt was limited to bombing of irrigation dikes in North Vietnam, or the use of tactical nuclear weapons, or a massive escalation in the numbers of American troops committed to the battle. The first two would have killed thousands of North Vietnamese indiscriminately and would have turned world opinion against the United States. The latter would have resulted in sharply increased American casualties and further divided the country, to say nothing of destroying any chance for diplomatic openings to the Soviets or Chinese. He ruled out a military victory in Vietnam. That left negotiations as the best way out but while negotiating, Nixon left no doubt that he would not cave in to North Vietnamese intransigence. In his inaugural address, President Nixon said; "To all those who would be tempted by weakness, let us leave no doubt that we will be as strong as we need be for as long as we need be."

Being strong on Vietnam and seeing the war through to a successful conclusion was complicated by domestic factors. The anti-war movement was becoming even more vocal and irrational in its opposition to American involvement. The liberal press weighted its reportage of the war strongly in favor of the enemy. As the most influential shaper of public opinion, televi-

(Above and Below) The 41st and 42nd Tactical Electronic Warfare Squadrons operated from Takhli RTAB as units of the 355th TFW. They provided jamming of NVA tracking and fire control radars with their EB-66s. (USAF)

sion news turned more and more Americans against the war with its literal reporting of battle scenes, bringing the carnage and suffering of war into American living rooms with the evening news. It became tougher and tougher to discern the higher moral purposes of the fight against communist totaliarianism when the fight and its grim consequences to the individuals doing the fighting were so graphically depicted, night after night. Not many news people were reminding the American public that the communists had slaughtered 50,000 innocents when they took over the north, or that they had killed over 3,000 civilians wantonly in their brief occupation of Hue during the Tet offensive. And public opinion was not the only impediment to being strong on Vietnam. Richard Nixon was the first president in 120 years to be elected without control of either house of congress being in the hands of his party.

(Above) A Huey from the 25th Infantry Division on a resupply mission at Chu Lai, RVN. It was the helicopter that enabled the allies to seize the initiative in the Vietnam War, and the Huey was the most prolific of all helicopters. (US Army)

(Below) A wounded Korean infantryman struggles to board a Dustoff medical evacuation Huey, as communist snipers fire at the hovering helicopter. Near Phan Rang, 1967. (Bell)

UH-1C Gunship of the 57th Assault Helicopter Company, 52nd Aviation Division at Phu Cat AB, October, 1970. (Norman E. Taylor)

Combat Assault! Troopers leap from a UH-1D Huey onto a landing zone in the Central Highlands of South Vietnam. (Bell)

Troopers from the 101st Airborne dropping to the landing zone from a UH-1D, which was prevented from landing by the stumps of trees blasted down in earlier fighting. (US Army)

Resupply mission in the Central Highlands, west of Kontum. The 4th Infantry Division caught and engaged a North Vietnamese unit, which was attempting to disengage and flee to Cambodia. Artillery and air strikes had effectively removed much of the jungle from this hill top, which then served as resupply landing zone. (Bell)

Troopers being extracted after a mission. (F.C. Brown)

UH-1C Gunship of the 57th Assault Helicopter Company landing at Phu Cat AB, 10 October, 1970. The 57th was activated 18 November, 1966 as the 236th Aviation Company, and became the 57th on 8 February, 1967. Its gunship platoon was known as "Cougars". (Norman E. Taylor)

UH-1D landing at Binh Chanh base camp, about 10 "Klicks" southwest of Saigon, July, 1967. Landing pad consists of a wood plank platform, necessary because of the ever-present mud during the rainy season. (Andy L. Mutzig)

29

2 1/2 ton truck from B Company, 7th Support Battalion, 199th Infantry Brigade. The UH-1D is assigned to the 199th, and sports the Brigade patch on it's nose. The truck is loaded with rubber fuel bladders and is probably refuelling the Huey. 81mm mortar in sandbagged gun position at left is used to fire illuminating rounds in case of a night attack. Binh Chanh base camp, July, 1967. (Andy L. Mutzig)

UH-1D making its approach and landing at the MACV Compound, Chau Phu City, RVN, during the monsoon season, 1970. (F.C. Brown)

UH-1D of the U.S. Army being directed aboard the battleship USS New Jersey (BB-62) by the Air Boss, Chief Warrant Officer Jacque E. Van Cleff, March 24, 1969. (US Navy)

Bell OH-58 Kiowa on the pad at the MACV Compound, Chau Phu City. The jeeps in the foreground belonged to Seabees and Milphap Tm. N-9. (F.C. Brown)

Army Hueys on the deck of USS New Jersey. The refurbished battleship provided fire support with it's sixteen inch guns, and Army commanders often visited in order to coordinate these fire missions. December 27, 1968. (US Navy)

Can Tho Airfield in the Delta, 1970. (F.C. Brown)

UH-1B of the 121st Assault Helicopter Company at Soc Trang, 1967. The gunship platoon was named "Viking Blue Diamond, Devils of the Delta". (Paul Murray via John Mastro)

Lockheed YO-3A was operated by the U.S. Army over South Vietnam. It was developed as a quiet reconnaissance aircraft, and whispered along on a wooden three bladed prop. (Bob Baldo)

(Above) OH-6A Loach landing at Phu Cat AB, 10 October, 1970. The OH-6 was used by Aero Scouts and was normally armed with a forward-firing 7.62MM minigun. Crew consisted of pilot and door gunner, who had a variety of personal weapons at his disposal. Loaches flew at low-level, and their crews collected more than their share of purple hearts. (Norman E. Taylor)

(Below) OV-1B Mohawk taxies out from the pad at Landing Zone English for a reconnaissance mission. The Mohawk gave the Army its fastest and most reliable source of battlefield intelligence. It carried a variety of intelligence gathering tools, including the SLAR (Side Looking Airborne Radar) shown here. (U.S. Army)

(Below) OV-1B of the 225th SAC, Tuy Hoa AB, photographed at Phu Cat AB on 18 November, 1970 by Norman E. Taylor.

USAF LT/COL Gene Levy (front) and Lt Bob Hand of the 12th TFW board their F-4C at Cam Ranh Bay AB, RVN for a December, 1968 mission against VC targets. (USAF)

F-4C of the 557th TFS, 12th TFW enroute to targets just north of the DMZ, as it prepares to take on fuel from a KC-135. (Norm Malayney)

F-105F "Fat Fanny" of the 333rd TFS, 355th TFW as it appeared in the Wild Weasel role, striking a SAM site.

1969

The North Vietnamese did not wait long to test the resolve of President Nixon. In February, 1969 they launched an offensive against the south. This resulted in immediate and sharply increased U.S. casualty figures. The new president met with his advisors to determine an appropriate course of action. General Ceighton Abrams, the U.S. Commander in Vietnam, and Ellsworth Bunker, U.S. Ambassador to South Vietnam, both recommended B-52 strikes against the communist sanctuaries in Cambodia, which had been logistical staging points and safe areas to regroup and plan new attacks for the communists. The Secretary of State and Secretary of Defense were both against the attacks, fearing that widening the war would intensify domestic dissent. But the President proposed to launch these attacks without making them public. He knew that the Cambodian leader, Prince Sihanouk, would welcome any action that would get the North Vietnamese out of his country, and would not criticize the bombings as long as they did not become public knowledge. He also knew that the North Vietnamese could not protest them without admitting to being in Cambodia...a presence they had steadastly denied. On March 17 the bombing of the Cambodian sanctuaries got underway. American casualties in South Vietnam immediately declined.

Throughout early 1969 President Nixon publically urged the North Vietnamese to negotiate in good faith, while continuing the pressure of bombing the Cambodian sanctuaries. In July he sent a letter to Ho Chi Minh via courier. He instructed the courier to say that, unless some progress was made by November 1, (which was the anniversary of the Johnson bombing halt) he

Victory belongs to the most perservering
Napoleon

would have to resort to "measures of great consequence and force." The letter itself was conciliatory and statesmanlike. President Nixon wrote;

I realize that it is difficult to communicate meaningfully across the gulf of four years of war. But precisely because of this gulf, I wanted to take this opportunity to reaffirm in all solemnity my desire to work for a just peace...

As I have said repeatedly, there is nothing to be gained by waiting...You will find us forthcoming and open-minded in a common effort to bring the blessings of peace to the brave people of Vietnam. Let history record that at this critical juncture, both sides turned their face toward peace rather than toward conflict and war.

Chinook at Vung Tau in September, 1969. It is adorned with various mission symbols. (Dave Evans)

The Boeing Vertol CH-47 Chinook provided the Army with it's basic heavy lift capability. It was powered by two turbine engines, ranging from 2,650 shp in the A model, to 3,750 shp in the C model. It could carry up to 44 troops, or 28,000lbs. of cargo. It is seen here about to begin placement of portable pontoon bridge sections. (U.S. Army)

Paratroopers of the 2nd Bn, 327th Inf, 1st Bg, 101st Airborne Division about to board Chinook for lift to Operation Klamath Falls, conducted around Bao Loc, March, 1968. (U.S. Army photo by SSG Al Wilson)

An Air Force C-123 Ranch Hand aircraft that was forced down after being hit by enemy ground fire is recovered by an Army CH-54. The CH-54 whose Army name was "Tarhe", but was known more familiarly by its civil name of "Skycrane" was powered by a pair of 4,500 shp turboshaft engines and was capable of lifting up to 20,000 lbs. (USAF)

CH-54 of the 1st Cavalry Division (Airmobile) hovers at Landing Zone "Laramie" at An Khe, RVN, February, 1968. Mountain top fire bases could only be resupplied by helicopter, and the CH-54's heavy lift capability was necessary to carry guns and ammo to these isolated outposts. (U.S. Army)

AH-1G Huey Cobra gunship from Battery B, 2nd Bn, 20th Artillery flying wing on a "Nighthawk" Huey in support of ground units of the First Cav, 1969. (U.S. Army)

Within a few days word came from North Vietnam requesting a secret meeting between Henry Kissinger, Nixon's national security advisor, and Xuan Thuy, the North Vietnamese negotiator. In this meeting, Kissinger reinterated President Nixon's desire to get the negotiations onto a more productive track, and his determination to take whatever actions necessary to convince the North Vietnamese of this. For their part, the North Vietnamese gave not an inch, maintaining their demands that all American troops be withdrawn from South Vietnam, President Thieu overthrown, and the NLF's ten points recognized before any negotiations could take place. They continued to insist that there were no North Vietnamese troops in South Viet-

nam.

Henry Cabot Lodge, a former ambassador to South Vietnam, had replaced Harriman and Vance at the Paris peace talks. After the meeting between Kissinger and Xuan Thuy he assumed a more aggressive stance in the American negotiating position.

In the meantime, the American withdrawl of troops had begun, with the first increment of 25,000 leaving in the spring of 1969, followed by a further 35,000 in December. The American negotiators made it clear to the North Vietnamese that they considered this a considerable concession, for which they expected some quid pro quo. None was forthcoming. The North Viet-

A-37s of the VNAF's 516th Fighter Squadron at the 'last chance' armament checkpoint at DaNang AB, September, 1970. (USAF photo by SSgt Andy Sarakon)

LAPES (Low Altitude Parachute Extraction System) was used to deliver supplies to landing zones too short, rough or hot to land on by the C-130.

A pair of A-37s over South Vietnam during their first combat mission in August, 1967. This was during the evaluation period for the A-37, and these aircraft carry an unusual Blue/Grey and White camouflage scheme. (USAF)

Crew chief of the Army's Cobra Transition School directing an AH-1G out of the bunker area at Vung Tau, September, 1970. (U.S. Army photo by SP-5 C.D. Turner)

AH-1G Cobra of B Company, 1st Aviation Battalion, 1st Infantry Division, whose call sign was "Rebels", often worked with OH-6 "Loach" scout helicopters in hunter-killer teams. The Rebels were a sister unit to the Confederate Air Force in Harlingen, Texas, hence the CAF wings on the tail boom.

Cobra of A Troop, 7th Squadron, 1st Cav over Kien Phong Province, October, 1969. (U.S. Army)

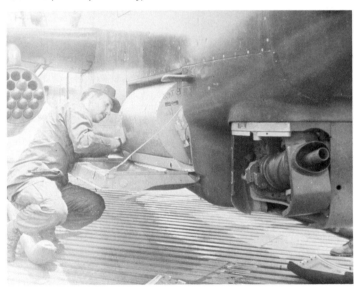

SP-4 Fred Palmer of Troop A, 7th Squadron, 17th Cav inspects the ammo drum of the 40mm grenade launcher of an AH-1G, July, 1970. (US Army)

AH-1G Cobra at the USARV Cobra Transition School at Vung Tau, September, 1970. It is armed with minigun and 40mm grenade launcher in the nose, along with 20mm Vulcan gun pods and seven shot rocket pods on the wings. (U.S. Army)

AH-1G of the 17th Cav with the XM-35 weapons system. The squadron nickname was "Undertakers", and this configuration (twin 40mm grenade launchers) was called a "Thumper Ship". (US Army)

namese were encouraged by the anti-war movement in the United States, feeling that it had brought one President down, and would do the same to this President if he dared to escalate the war. President Nixon addressed this hope in a news conference in September when he acknowledged the public protests that had occurred and were threatened, but vowed that he would not be affected by them in his actions directed at ending the war. Nevertheless, the anti-war movement, with the support of an increasingly hostile press, effectively negated Nixon's ultimatum to the North Vietnamese. The very people who professed to want the war ended, by their actions had prolonged it by encouraging the enemy to maintain his rigid posture in the negotiations.

The President had announced a major foreign policy speech on November 3, just two days past his announced deadline to the North Vietnamese. Most of the liberal press in the United States predicted that the speech would announce unilateral cease-fire on large scale troop pull-outs from Vietnam. Their speculation was based upon the October 15 Moratorium which saw 250,000 anti-war protestors invade Washington D.C. They felt that no Presi-

CH-54 lifting an A-1 from the grass alongside the runway at Nakhon Phanom after battle damage resulted in a wheels-up landing of the Spad.

dent could ignore such pressure. They underestimated Mr. Nixon, whose perspective was much more realistic, and who said so in a public response to a letter castigating him for effectively ignoring the protest. He said; "If a President — any President — allowed his course to be set by those who demonstrate, he would betray the trust of all the rest. Whatever the issue, to allow government policy to be made in the streets would destroy the democratic process. It would give the decision, not to the majority, and not to those with the strongest arguments, but to those with the loudest voices...It would allow every group to test its strength not at the ballot box but through confrontation in the streets."

In his November 3 speech President Nixon reaffirmed his determination to see the war through to a just and satisfactory conclusion, and pointed out that he had advanced his peace initiative. It was the North Vietnamese that were determined to attain victory through military means. The President told his audience that that was not possible if the American people were united. The communists could not defeat America — only Americans could do that. He appealed to the great "silent majority" of Americans to show their support for his efforts to end the war.

When the speech ended, the major media immediately set about tearing it

apart, telling their audience what the President should have said, and how much trouble he was now in because he had not caved in to the liberal line. Public opinion, however, was solidly behind the President. Thousands of telegrams, letters, and phone calls flooded the White House pledging support for the President. Public opinion polls showed that 77% of the public was in favor of the policy of the President on Vietnam, and he received his highest overall approval rating, 68%, in the week following the speech. It was a rebuff that the liberal press would not forgive...or forget.

The President's commitment to stay in Vietnam until a just and honorable peace had been won, coupled with the overwhelming public support for his decision, was answer enough to the North Vietnamese. They now knew that they could not scare Richard Nixon into capitulation. Many bloody battles remained to be fought before the United States ended its role in the Vietnam War.

Lt Glenn Cloes climbs down from "Lead Zeppelin", an F-105D of the 355th TFW, after a 1970 combat mission, Takhli RTAB.

(Below) The late Daniel "Chappie" James, as he appeared while deputy Wing CO of the 8th TFW, 1967. James was a Colonel at this time, though he later rose to four star rank in the USAF. He was deputy to Colonel Robin Olds, one of the most popular combat leaders in USAF history. They were sometimes known as "Black Man and Robin".

Colonel Robin Olds, C.O. of the 8th TFW, checks the vintage in preparation of celebrating one of his four Mig kills.

A-1H of the VNAF's 514th Fighter Squadron, at Tan Son Nhut AB, 14 December, 1970. (Norman E. Taylor)

'Patricia Lynn' RB-57E of Detachment 1, 460th TRW taxies for takeoff from Tan Son Nhut AB, December, 1970. The RB-57E served for eight continuous years in the Vietnam War, from 1963 to 1971. They carried a variety of reconnaissance equipment, including oblique and panoramic cameras, and infra-red photography equipment. 54-245 flew the second combat mission of the war for the RB-57Es, and had amassed 8,000 hours flying time before being withdrawn in 1971. A special citation was awarded the Patricia Lynn unit by MACV in 1970, "for providing 94% of the battlefield intelligence during the war to date". That was getting the maximum benefit from a unit that had no more than five aircraft assigned at any one time. (Norman E. Taylor, Above and Lex McAulay, Left)

U.S. Navy OP-2E Neptune engaged in project Igloo White, in which Air Delivered Seismic Detection Sensors (ADSID) were dropped on the Ho Chi Minh Trail in Laos and Cambodia to aid intelligence in pin-pointing the heaviest traffic for fighters and gunships assigned to hit targets on the trail. OP-2s operated from Nakhon Phanom AB, Thailand, alternately known as "NKP" or "Naked Fanny" to the crews. (USAF photo by SSgt Alton G. Gaston)

Vietnamization

While Presidents Johnson and Kennedy had both paid lip service to the necessity for the Vietnamese to fight their own battles, it was Richard Nixon who finally implemented this strategy. Some of the anti-war critics thought that Vietnamization should have taken place much sooner than it actually did, but that was not possible for a variety of reasons. The South Vietnamese did not have the capacity to accept the huge amounts of military aid necessary to fend off the communists in 1965. Their armed forces were just not organized for the kind of war they would have to fight to defeat the communists. The fact that we were able to begin turning over vast quantities of sophisticated military hardware to the South Vietnamese, beginning in 1969, spoke volumes for how well they had learned to use this equipment.

Vietnamization did not just happen by accident. Nguyen Cao Ky had been urging that the South Vietnamese be given more responsibility for their own destinies for sometime, and his pleas finally bore fruit with the Nixon Administration. More than 12,000 Vietnamese Officers attended the Command and General Staff College at Fort Leavenworth, Kansas; Vietnamese soliders were attending basic training classes in the United States; and thousands of Vietnamese pilots got their training in the continental U.S. The South Vietnamese armed forces had grown from 250,000 to 427,000 regulars from 1965 to 1968. By the end of 1970 they would have 1,100,000 men under arms, which included the regional and provisional forces ("Ruff Puffs", as they

Failure is more frequently from want of energy than want of capital.

Daniel Webster

were called by the Americans, were the equivalent of Revolutionary War minutemen...villagers who were trained to drop their farm implements and grab their weapons when their villages were threatened by the VC).

The American withdrawal from Vietnam began in 1969. At this time there was no schedule for complete withdrawal, since the pace of Vietnamization was dependent upon communist reaction to this new program. A complete withdrawl of American forces was not comtemplated, since it was felt that it would be necessary to maintain some logistical support facilities for the maintenance of certain equipment. Even as it began, many American field commanders felt that Vietnamization was a risky venture. The prevailing opinion was that ARVN would be able to deal with the Viet Cong, but they would need a lot of help to hold their own against regular North Vietnamese units.

The American strategy included maintaining a significant aerial presence, including B-52s and tactical fighters, for as long as it took to assure the continued survival of South Vietnam. Airlift capacity was to be the domain of the VNAF, with over 1,100 aircraft and helicopters turned over during Vietnamization. This was just one incidence of the lavish transferral of arms, which would finally have unforseen consequences. Not many South Vietnamese leaders were considering what would happen when all of the Americans were gone, while their expensive-to-operate weaponry remained

AC-47D of the Vietnam Air Force (VNAF), assigned to the 314th Special Missions Squadron, based at Tan Son Nhut. December, 1970. (Norman E. Taylor)

C-47B of the 415th Transport Squadron, 33rd Wing, VNAF at Tan Son Nhut, December, 1970. (Norman E. Taylor)

C-47B of the 415th Transport Squadron, 33rd Wing, VNAF at Tan Son Nhut, December, 1970. (Norman E. Taylor)

C-119G of the 413th Transport Squadron, 53rd Tactical Wing, taxies at Tan Son Nhut, December, 1970. VNAF was the only service to operate the transport version of the Flying Boxcar in Vietnam. (Norman E. Taylor)

(Left) VNAF pilot straps into a F-5C of the 522 Squadron, 23rd Tactical Wing at Bien Hoa AB, RVN, July, 1968. The F-5 was the first jet operated on a large scale by VNAF. (USAF via Norm E. Taylor)

F-5s of the 522nd with a load of napalm and 500lb bombs on a mission in support of ARVN troops. Checkerboard stripe on fuselage was Black and Yellow. (USAF via Norman E. Taylor)

The ubiquitous Huey was used by ARVN, which began to assume a larger and larger share of the lift duties as Vietnamization progressed. Here seen at Tan Son Nhut in December, 1970. The "packs" in the foreground are actually main and reserve parachutes belonging to an ARVN airborne unit, lined up prior to boarding a transport aircraft. (Norman E. Taylor)

behind, Ky was one who did, and he warned Thieu; "Don't imagine we will have the same kind of firepower as we have now when the Americans leave." The problem was, ARVN was being taught to fight a war in the American way, using ammunition unstintingly to save lives. But in 1970 there were still over 400,000 Americans in Vietnam, and there was little reason to doubt the seriousness of the American long-term commitment to the South Vietnamese cause. In fact, it was the perceived legitimacy of this commitment, now embodied in a Vietnamization program that seemed to be working, that led the North Vietnamese to even bolder military adventures. Vietnamization was an idea whose time had come, and it worked amazingly well with direct American assistance. It worked so well that by 1972 American troop strength was down to 60,000. But after so many years of having Americans explain

how to do things, then doing them themselves, the Vietnamese were bound to be less aggressive than their instructors. It would be a race against time to see if the necessary aggressiveness could be instilled in ARVN before all of the Americans were gone.

A-7A of VA-147 "Argonauts" on final approach to the USS Ranger VA-47 was the first unit to fly the Corsair II in combat.

A-4F Skyhawk of VA-93 about to recover aboard USS Bon Homme Richard after a 1970 mission over Vietnam.

The Marines used the TA-4F as a fast FAC aircraft, armed with 2.75 white phosporous rockets to mark targets for their F-4's and A-4's.

'Seawolf' Hueys of the Navy's HAL-3 operated in the Mekong Delta as part of Operation Game Warden, a subsidiary program of the wide ranging Operation Market Time interdiction of VC seaborne arms shipments. (U.S. Navy)

Lt. Jim Hurley, of VF-143 flying a BARCAP mission off the carrier Constellation. The F-4J is loaded for max duration, with three external fuel tanks, and only a pair of Sidewinder AAMs. (via Jim Hurley)

VNAF Huey from the 211th Helicopter Squadron lifts off after dropping ARVN troops on a combat assault in the Mekong Delta, July, 1970. (USAF)

VNAF personnel of the 514th Fighter Squadron refuel and rearm A-1Hs prior to a mission from Tan Son Nhut, November, 1970. The Spad continued to carry the bulk of the close air support missions for VNAF throughout the 1967-70 period. (Norman E. Taylor)

(Bottom) A-1H of the 514th Squadron, 23rd Tactical Wing returning to Tan Son Nhut after a mission. The 23rd was based at Bien Hoa, but often flew missions from Tan Son Nhut when a high level of activity put a strain on the facilities at Bien Hoa. (Norman E. Taylor)

(Below) A-1H of the 514th Squadron, armed with 8 500lb bombs, at Tan Son Nhut December, 1970. (Norman E. Taylor)

Start up at Bien Hoa, July, 1969. Vietnamization was built upon American tactics, with American largess, as evidenced by the heavy load of ordnance on this Skyraider. (USAF)

A-1H of the 514th Fighter Squadron, formerly belonged to USAF 56th Special Operations Wing at Nakhon Phanom. Photographed at Tan Son Nhut December, 1970 by Norm Taylor.

23rd Tactical Wing used this O-1 to control many of its Skyraider close support missions. Bien Hoa AB, RVN 15 April, 1970. (USAF)

The U-17 (Military version of the Cessna 180) was used in psychological warfare by the NVAF 23rd Tactical Wing, dropping leaflets and making broadcasts from special speakers. Bien Hoa AB, RVN, 15 April, 1970. (USAF)

(Lower Middle Left) The U-6A Beaver was used by the 33rd Tactical Wing of the VNAF for reconnaissance, administrative, and psychological warfare duties. Tan Son Nhut AB, RVN, January, 1968. (Norman E. Taylor)

(Above) The Beavers of the VNAF 33rd Wing carried a distinctive Green/Tan camouflage scheme, as well as the wing badge on the engine cowl. (USAF)

(Left) U-17A of the 14th Liason Squadron, 62nd Tactical Wing of VNAF at Nha Trang, August, 1969. (Norman E. Taylor)

RA-5C Reconnaissance Vigilante of RVAH-5 about to be launched from USS Kitty Hawk.

F-8E Crusaders from VF-53 inbound to North Vietnam in March, 1967. (U.S. Navy)

USS Kitty Hawk (CVA-63) in the South China Sea during its 1969 deployment to WESTPAC. Aboard is Air Group 11, with F-4s (VF-213, 114), A-6s (VA-65), A-7s (VA-37, 192), A-3s, RA-5s, E-2s, and H-2. (U.S. Navy)

(Above) USS Coral Sea (CVA-43) during its 1969-70 Westpac cruise. November 1969. Air Group 15 is aboard with F-4s (VF-11, 151), A-6s (VA-152), A-7s (VA-86, 82), C1, E-2, and A-3. (U.S. Navy)

(Left Middle) USS Oriskany (CVA-34) underway in the South China Sea, July 19, 1969, with Air Group 16 aboard. Aircraft included F-8s (VF-194, 195) A-4s (VA-195, 162, 164) A-3B (VAH-4), E-1B (VAW-12). (US Navy)

(Left) Reconnaissance mission preparing to launch from Ranger. Though the RA-5 was a fast recon platform, it was not manueverable, and visibility from the cockpit was not the greatest. It was often escorted by MIGCAP F-4s. December 13, 1967. (U.S. Navy)

(Above) F-4B at the moment the catapult has begun its forward stroke to launch the Phantom from the deck of Ranger in the Gulf of Tonkin, December, 1967. (U.S. Navy)

(Below) Attaching a Phantom to the cat aboard Connie, 1969. VF-142 Ghostriders operated the F-4B as a part of Air Group 14. (Jim Hurley)

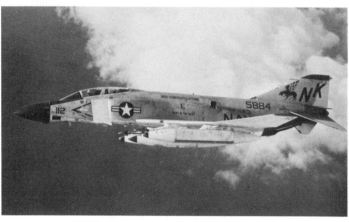

(Above) F-4J of VF-143 off the USS Constellation, 1969. (Jim Hurley)

(Right) Photo taken from the starboard forward elevator of Coral Sea, showing the foreward section of the island, including the bridge.

(Below) USAF KC-135s provided supplementary refuelling capacity to Navy strike aircraft. Because the Navy uses the probe and drogue method of refuelling, while the Air Force had standarized with receptacle in the receiving aircraft, the KC-135 was fitted with the drogue prior to these missions. (USAF)

1970

War hath no fury like a non-combatant.
C.E. Montague — Disenchantment

From a media point of view, the most memorable event of 1970 was the flare-up of anti-war protests that occurred as a result of the Cambodian incursion. As was so often the case during the Vietnam War, the media siezed on the unimportant aspects of this story, ignoring the major reason for the incursion, and how it would affect the course of the war in the future.

As 1970 began the North Vietnamese were moving substantial numbers of troops and huge quantites of equipment and weaponry into Cambodia. The apparent success of Vietnamization had prompted the communists to prepare for renewed heavy attacks on American and South Vietnamese installations. They were still playing to the American domestic audience, feeling that if they could inflict heavy casualties on the Americans, they would accelerate the withdrawal of U.S. troops. And, if they could do the same to the South Vietnamese, they would slow down Vietnamization and possibly cause irreparable harm to the emerging sense of confidence within ARVN. President Nixon's November speech had hardened American public opinion on the war, and the communists worried about losing what they felt had been substantial American sympathy for their position. In addition, they were aware that the Nixon Administration was carrying on talks with their two major patrons, the Russians and Chinese.

Henry Kissinger had been continuing his secret meetings with the North Vietnamese in Paris, and though they remained as intransigent as ever in their professed position, Kissinger thought he saw them weakening slightly. He thought that there was a real possibility of progress, perhaps even a breakthrough by April. The North Vietnamese, for their part, continued to prepare for an all-out assault.

Then, on March 18 a bloodless coup overthrew the Cambodian head of state Prince Norodhem Sihanouk, who was visting Moscow at the time. President Nixon's advisors counseled restraint, feeling that the new Cambodian government of General Lon Nol, a strong anti-communist, was not strong enough to survive. But Lon Nol's troops fought well against the communists, and closed the routes from Sihanoukville to the communist sanctuaries. Sihanoukville was Cambodia's deep water port, and the North Vietnamese had taken advantage of its proximity to their Cambodian staging areas by shipping much of their supplies through the port. The government under Sihanouk had been unwilling or unable to stop this flagrant violation of their neutrality.

When Kissinger met with the North Vietnamese following the coup, they blamed the United States for engineering the coup and refused to make any commitment to the peace process. Kissinger recommended, and Nixon agreed, that the talks be suspended indefinitely. The diplomatic channel was dormant. It was now just a matter of time until the fighting intensified to reflect the massive logistic efforts of the communists. To almost everyone's surprise, it was not the communists who took the initiative.

After announcing that 150,000 American troops would be withdrawn from Vietnam within the following year — an announcement that temporarily defused the anti-war movement. President Nixon decided that something would have to be done about the communist sanctuaries in Cambodia. Not only were they a threat to the Americans, now standing down and preparing to leave the country, they were an active threat to the Lon Nol government, who, despite a gallant defense, was losing more and more territory.

The sanctuaries were in two main areas. Parrot's Beak, a small peninsula

Ordnance crewman aboard Kitty Hawk preparing to load bombs aboard attack aircraft prior to mission against North Vietnam. (U.S. Navy)

(Left and Below) Handling Snakeye bombs aboard Oriskany (Left) and fusing 500 pounders loaded on an A-6A aboard America. (Below) (U.S. Navy)

(Above) Skyhawks from VA-93 preparing to launch from USS Hancock (CVA-19) for a mission against North Vietnam. It was Hancock's practice to keep a pair of each type of fighter and attack aircraft loaded and on alert status. 31 May, 1967. (U.S. Navy)

A-4E of VA-163, off Oriskany, diverted to Cam Ranh Bay after a mission over South Vietnam in 1967. (Neal Schneider via R.M. Hill)

A-6 Intruder of VA-196 coming aboard Constellation after a mission over North Vietnam on July 6, 1968. (U.S. Navy)

of Cambodian land which stabs into South Vietnam, was just 33 miles from Saigon; and the Fishhook, a curved piece of Cambodian real estate that projects into South Vietnam fifty miles northwest of Saigon. Both contained massive amounts of communist war material. Intelligence also indicated that COSVN — the Central Office of South Vietnam — the communist headquarters, was located in the Fishhook. Since a large South Vietnamese Army presence was in the border area directly opposite Parrot's Beak, it was decided that ARVN would attack those sanctuaries. The Fishhook would be hit two days later by a joint force of U.S. and ARVN troops.

The ARVN operation got underway on April 29, and was immediately attacked by the anti-war faction in the United States, who urged the Administration to disavow any support for the attacks. Imagine their chagrin then, when the President, not only did not disavow the attack, but announced that U.S. forces would take part in another incursion into Cambodia. In a nationally televised speech, President Nixon explained the strategic importance of the Cambodian sanctuaries, and how their impunity from attack was making the American withdrawal and peace negotiations impossible. He further promised that all troops would be withdrawn as soon as the North Vietnamese troops had been driven out of Cambodia and their equipment captured or destroyed. But the most telling line from the whole speech...a line which would echo like a death knell for U.S. foreign policy for years to come...was this; "If, when the chips are down, the world's most powerful nation, the United States of America, acts like a pitiful, helpless giant, the forces of totalitarianism and anarchy will threaten free nations and free institutions throughout the world."

Nevertheless, there was a storm of protest from the anti-war movement, and from left-leaning Senators and Congressmen, whose irrational response

Ordnance men aboard USS Kitty Hawk loading a multiple ejector rack (MER) with six 500lb bombs onto an A-6 of VA-75. May, 1967. (U.S. Navy)

to the Cambodian incursion demonstrated their inadequacy. Such Democrat stalwarts as Edmund Muskie, Walter Mondale, and George McGovern were the most strident in their criticism. It took a British publication, The Economist, to put the whole operation into perspective. They wrote; "It is not the Americans who have brought the war to Cambodia, but the communists. For years, North Vietnam has violated the neutrality of this country — with barely a chirp of protest from the rest of the world...To condemn the United States for 'invading' neutral Cambodia is about as rational as to condemn Britain for 'invading' formally neutral Holland in 1944."

The wave of student activism that had swept American college campuses in the 1960's, had been channeled into anti-war, anti-establishment — anti-almost-everything-about-accepted-norms-of-modern-life-in-these-United States — by 1970 erupted into violence on several campuses. Bombings and arson came to many colleges, including Kent State in Ohio where demonstrators burned the ROTC building down. The Governor of Ohio called out the National Guard to restore order and ensure that the University would remain open. He called the demonstrators "worse than Brownshirts." On May 4, these "Brownshirts" attacked a small group of Guardsmen with rocks, surrounding them and driving them to the top of a small hill. Something — some spark — ignited the pent-up emotions of the Guardsmen, who opened fire on the students. Two protestors and two bystanders were killed.

VA-85 Intruder carries a cryptic message ("Look Worm Another 4 Tons") on one of its 500lb bombs. It is taxiing to the cat aboard USS America (CVA-66) prior to a June 1, 1968 mission. (U.S. Navy)

The reaction to the Kent State shooting was a paroxysm of campus violence and vandalism that shocked and disgusted most Americans. The majority of these demonstrators were woefully ignorant of the issues, and were indulging youthful impulses to challenge authority. A few were pathologically violent. The majority of Americans supported the steps being taken by President Nixon to end the war. The New York Building and Construction Trades Council sponsored a parade to City Hall to demonstrate their support. Their ire had been raised after New York Mayor John Lindsay ordered the flag at City Hall flown at half staff as part of "a day of reflection" after the tradgedy at Kent State. This led to the famous confrontation between the "hard hats" and the anti-war demonstrators.

The scoreboard for the Cambodian operations leaves no doubt that it was not only militarily sound, but also necessary to save allied lives. It was easily the most successful operation of the war to that point, with more arms, ammunition, equipment, and food captured within a month than had been captured in all of 1969. Enough individual weapons to equip seventy four full strength North Vietnames battalions were captured. Enough rice to feed every communist in South Vietnam for four months was captured. 143,000 rocket, mortar, and recoilless rifle rounds were captured. And 199,552 anti-

A-6 from VA-196 about to launch from Connie on November 15, 1968. It is loaded with Shrike and Standard ARM missiles for a strike against SAM sites. (U.S. Navy)

(Top Right) VA-56 Corsair IIs off the Ranger on 18 December 1969. During the bombing halt missions were flown against targets in South Vietnam and Laos. (U.S. Navy)

(Above Left) A-7A of VA-86 about to be launched from Coral Sea while enroute to WESTPAC. The air group maintained its skills during the long transition to the war zone by conducting air operations daily. (U.S. Navy)

(Left) A-7 being attached to the catapult shuttle aboard Coral Sea. The A-7 incorporated the catapult attach bar in the nose landing gear, doing away with the cables used on earlier carrier aircraft. 20 December 1969. (U.S. Navy)

(Below) The first Navy squadron to operate the A-7 Corsair II was VA-147, off the USS Ranger. CAG airplane is about to launch on a mission to suppress SAM sites in North Vietnam. It is loaded with Shrike radar-homing missile and CBUs. January, 1968. (U.S. Navy)

One of the most daring chapters in the history of the Vietnam War occured in November, 1970 when an American force raided the North Vietnamese prison camp at Son Tay, just 23 miles from Hanoi, in an effort to rescue 61 American POWs who had been held there. Unfortunately, the POWs had been moved before the raiders arrived. Nevertheless, the raiders proved the ability to penetrate NVA defense, wreak havoc within an enemy installation, and escape without suffering a single casualty. (USAF)

aircraft rounds, 5,482 mines, 62,022 grenades, 83,000 pounds of explosives, 435 vehicles, and 11,688 bunkers or fighting positions were destroyed. By any reckoning, it was a major setback for the communists...a fact which was borne out by the sharply reduced casualty figures in the weeks following the Cambodian incursion (93 per week in the six months preceding the operation, 51 per week in the six months following).

Was the President hailed as an astute leader, who was willing to take big political chances in order to save the lives of American troops? Was he congratulated for the success of this operation? Far from it. The leftward media continued to castigate him for violating Cambodian neutrality and for 'widening' the war. The Senate, which had become a rooting section for the North Vietnamese, passed the Cooper Church amendment, whose effect was to require the President to withdraw all American troops from Cambodia by July 1. From a practical standpoint, this was meaningless, since all troops had been withdrawn before the amendment was passed. But it did signal the burgeoning willingness of the Congress to intrude upon what had previously been the exclusive province of the President. They would now presume to make foreign policy, even to dictating strategy in the war, without the

A-7 follows an A-3 off the deck of the USS America for an October, 1968 mission against North Vietnam. Misions were restricted to areas below the 20th paralell until just before the election, when LBJ stopped all bombing of North Vietnam in an effort to get the communists to negotiate an end to the war. (U.S. Navy)

necessary knowledge. It was an ominous portent of things to come.

The peace negotiations in Paris had broken down, with the North Vietnamese insisting upon deposition of President Thieu before they would negotiate seriously. President Nixon, feeling that the Cambodian operation had deprived the North Vietnamese of the ability to mount a major offensive during the forseeable future, proposed a peace plan which effectively silenced the anti-war movement. This sweeping proposal, put forth publically on October 7, included a cease-fire in place, followed by a negotiated peace and withdrawal of all foreign troops after POWs had been exchanged. He followed this up with an announcement of the withdrawal of 40,000 American troops before Christmas. The North Vietnamese ignored this plan and continued to fight, although at a reduced rate.

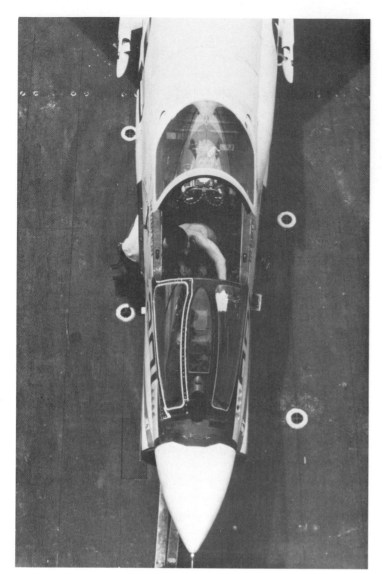

Catapult Officer aboard USS Oriskany signals the pilot of a VF-162 Crusader to advance his throttle to full power in preparation for a cat shot from the number one catapult. August, 1967. (U.S. Navy)

(Left) A plane captain cleans the windscreen of an F-8 Crusader aboard USS Bon Homme Richard. (CVA-31) (U.S. Navy)

Crusader of VF-162 "Hunters" returning to Oriskany after a December, 1967 mission over North Vietnam. The F-8 was used on the smaller aircraft carriers, which were unable to operate the bigger, heavier F-4 Phantom. It was the last of the single-engine, single place Navy fighters, and was at its best as a clear air mass air-to-air fighter. (U.S. Navy)

(Above) Ensign Bob Walters performing preflight checks in the cockpit of his VF-162 Crusader prior to a September, 1967 mission against North Vietnam from Oriskany. (U.S. Navy)

(Left) Loading AIM-9 Sidewinder AAMs on an F-8 aboard USS Hancock prior to a May, 1967 mission. The Crusader carried up to four of the heat seeking missiles, and was armed with four M-61 20mm cannon in the fuselage. It could also carry air to ground rockets and bombs, and was occasionally employed in the attack role. (U.S. Navy)

Crusaders from VF-24 and VF-211 are prepared for launch from Bonnie Dick for a 3 March 1967 mission against North Vietnam. F-8s from CVW-21 accounted for a dozen Mig kills. (U.S. Navy)

Deck crewmen rushing to assist the pilot of a VF-53 Crusader whose nose gear collapsed on landing aboard Bon Homme Richard, August, 1968. (U.S. Navy)

F-8E of VF-53 prepares for launch from (CVA-31) for a May, 1968, air-to-ground mission. (U.S. Navy)

F-8 landing aboard USS Hancock after a May, 1967 mission against North Vietnam. The Migs were very active that month, and six were shot down by U.S. aircraft. Five fell to F-8s and one to an A-4. (U.S. Navy)

(Left) RF-8A photo Crusader from VFP-63 milliseconds from being slung off the number two cat of USS Oriskany. (U.S. Navy)

F-8 accelerating down the catapult track aboard USS Bon Homme Richard for an April, 1967 mission. (U.S. Navy)

RA-5C of RVAH-5 off Constellation enroute to a 700 KM/H photo pass over North Vietnam, in the company of one F-4 escort, 1968. Reconnaissance assets became so important in keeping track of NVA movements after the bombing halt of 1968 that the production line for the RA-5 Vigilante was reopened, and a further 40 aircraft produced. The RF-8 Crusader was modernized to RF-8G standards and continued to serve until after the end of United States involvement. (Jim Hurley)

E-1B Tracer Airborne Early Warning aircraft launching from USS Coral Sea (CVA-43) for a January, 1968 mission over the Gulf of Tonkin. (U.S. Navy)

F-8 Crusader of VF-53 about to break into the landing pattern over Bonnie Dick after a June, 1970 mission. (U.S. Navy)

Grumman E-2 Hawkeye from VAW-16. The E-2 gave the fleet greater battlefield surveillance capability. (U.S. Navy)

(Left) E-2B from VAW 113 recovering aboard Constellation after a 1969 mission. The E-2 became operational in 1965, with VAW-11. The rotodome above the fuselage is the antenna from the AN/APS-96 radar. It revolves at 6 rpm and can be lowered 2 feet for stowage on the hangar deck. By 1971 all E-2A's had been upgraded to E-2B standards, which included installation of a Litton L-304 microelectronic general-purpose computer. (Jim Hurley)

Grumman C-2A Greyhound, Carrier On-board Delivery (COD) aircraft. The C-2 was developed using many of the same components used in the E-2. (Shinichi Ohtaki)

An SH-3A Sea King patrol helicopter refuelling from the Destroyer USS Steinake (DD-863) during Operation Sea Dragon in the Gulf of Tonkin. September, 1968. (U.S. Navy)

Plane guard helicopter from HC-1, being readied for takeoff prior to landing of F-4Js after a mission over Vietnam, 1968. The UH-2 Seasprite flew abeam the carrier during launch and recovery, alert for aircraft that might end up in the water, or for men overboard from the carrier. (Jim Hurley)

A flight deck crewman directs an SH-34 Seahorse aboard USS Okinawa. The H-34 was one of the first helicopters to see combat in Southeast Asia and continued in a variety of utility roles with the Navy and Marines throughout most of the sixties. October, 1967. (U.S. Navy)

(Above) VAP-61 and 62 flew camouflaged RA-3B reconnaissance versions of the venerable A-3 Skywarrior. Operating from Danang, RVN and Don Muang RTAB, the RA-3s provided surveillance along the Ho Chi Minh Trail with their infrared and video real-time cameras. Working with attack aircraft from the carrier air groups, the RA-3s "fingered" the truck traffic for the bombers during the night, when they were moving, and during the day, when they were in hiding. they also carried COIR (camouflage detection) film, which could detect the difference between living and dead foliage, thereby spotlighting camouflaged truck parks. (Shinichi Ohtaki)

(Left) An EKA-3B of Tactical Electronics Carrier Special Squadron 130 (VAG-130) on a June, 1970 mission from Bonnie Dick. The Skywarrior also served in the airborne jamming role. (U.S. Navy)

(Below, Left) VAH-123 A-3 coming aboard. The A-3 Skywarrior was known more familiarly as the "Whale", a reference to its size. With its relatively close tracked landing gear, it could provide some exciting moments during recovery aboard a carrier. (U.S. Navy)

(Below) A view of the A-3 Skywarrior as tanker, still another role played well by the big attack bomber. July 1967, off the USS Hancock. (U.S. Navy)

(Top) EKA-3B Skywarrior approaching a USAF KC-135 tanker over Southeast Asia 26 April, 1968. (USAF)

(Above) A-3B of VAH-4 refuelling an RA-5C of RVAH-11 after a mission over North Vietnam, January, 1968. Both off USS Kitty Hawk. (U.S. Navy)

(Right) The A-1 Skyraider continued to be a mainstay of the attack squadrons on the smaller aircraft carriers into 1967. This A-1H is armed with rocket pods for a 1967 mission. (Tom Hansen via R.M. Hill)

Bell SK-5 Patrol Air Cushion Vehicle (PACV) along the My Tho river December, 1967. The 60 mph PACVs were a part of Operation Game Warden, designed to interdict supplies bound for Viet Cong guerillas in the Mekong Delta. (U.S. Navy)

Crewmen rearming a Uh-1B Huey of Light Helicopter Attack Squadron Three (HAL-3) The Navy began using the Huey gunship in 1966, as another part of Market Time and Game Warden. (U.S. Navy)

Huey gunship of HAL-3 lifts from USS Harnett County (LST-821) on a mission to support Navy patrol boats in the Mekong Delta, November, 1967. (U.S. Navy)

The right door gunner of a HAL-3 Huey prepares for a firing run on a Viet Cong ambush site in the Delta. The Huey was answering a distress call from the PBR visible just over the barrel of the top machine gun. The PBR is still smoking from a VC recoilless rifle round it had taken only minutes before. May, 1968. (U.S. Navy)

UH-1D of HAL-3, which dubbed themselves "Seawolf", lifting off from Vinh Long for a January, 1967 mission. (U.S. Navy)

Landing Signal Enlisted man directs the pilot of a UH-1E aboard the Amphibious Transport Dock USS Cleveland (LPD-7) October, 1969. (U.S. Navy)

Seawolf Huey firing a rocket in support of PBRs of River Section 523 on the Co Chien River, 50 miles south of Saigon, October, 1969. (U.S. Navy)

A pair of VAL-4 "Black Ponies" OV-10s enroute to targets in South Vietnam.

(Right) Aviation Machinist's Mate Airman Jack L. Riley draining a fuel sump during preflight inspection of one of VAL-4s Broncos prior to a mission. (U.S. Navy)

OV-10A Bronco of Light Attack Squadron Four (VAL-4) takes off from Vung Tau loaded with rocket pods. The OV-10 was developed during the early sixties when DOD planners were enamored of the conter-insurgency role. It was eventually adopted by the Marine Corps and USAF. The Navy flew it in the light strike role, while USAF and Marines used it as a FAC and light observation aircraft.

The Flight Director aboard the Amphibious Transport Dock USS Duluth (LPD-6) brings in an H-53 to airlift a 105MM howitzer to Marines in the I Corps area of South Vietnam. (U.S. Navy)

(Top Right) CH-53 placing a 105MM howitzer of the 12th Marine Regiment into a fire base position southwest of An Hoa during Operation Taylor Common in 1968. (U.S. Marines)

(Bottom Right) The huge rotor blades of the CH-53 creates heavy downwash as the Marine helicopter prepares to lift a howitzer to Marines in South Vietnam. (U.S. Navy)

CH-53A at the Marble Mountain Air Base, RVN. (USAF)

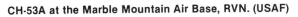

UH-1E Gunship at Marble Mountain, armed with a CBU-55. (Fuel Air Explosive) in December, 1970. (U.S. Navy)

(Below) The EF-10B continued in service into the late 60's, here seen at Ubon RTAB, December, 1968. (Al Piccirillo via Norm Taylor)

CH-46 resupplying Echo Company, 2nd Battalion, 7th Marines during Operation Oklahoma Hills, 17 April, 1969. (U.S. Marines)

(Below) Seabees of U.S. Naval Mobile Construction Battalion 58 work on the parking apron at the Air Freight Terminal, Chu Lai, RVN. An F-4 of VMFA-232 has just returned from a mission. April, 1969. (U.S. Navy)

VMFA-115 operated its F-4s from Chu Lai, which with the aid of SATS became one of the largest jet bases in northern South Vietnam. This F-4B was photographed during a September, 1968 visit to Ubon RTAB. (Al Piccirillo via Norm Taylor)

F-4B of VMFA-115 takes off from Chu Lai for a May, 1967 mission. (U.S. Marines)

(Below) F-4Bs of VMFA-542, MAG 11, 1st MAW out of Danang on a close support mission. (U.S. Marines)

F-4B of VMFA-122 landing at Danang after a mission in support of Marine ground troops. Its armament configuration is notable for the carrying of both Sparrow and Sidewinder AAMs, air-to-air weapons seldom used by Marine aircraft in Southeast Asia. (U.S. Marines)

(Left) VMFA-122 Phantom with the unusual loading of three 20MM Vulcan gatling gun pods. Each of these could be set to fire at cyclic rates of up to 6,000 rounds per minute.

(Bottom Left) A-6A of VMA (AW) 242 rotating from the runway at Chu Lai enroute to targets in South Vietnam. It is armed with decidedly vintage 2,000lb bombs. January, 1967. (U.S. Marines)

(Below) EA-6A of VMCJ-1 refuelling at Danang, January, 1970. The first Marine A-6 squadron in Vietnam, VMCJ-1 continued to provide airborne jamming for strike aircraft throughout the late 60's. (U.S. Marines)

A-6A of VMA(AW)-255 at the "last chance" checkpoint, where safety pins are removed and armament is checked, prior to takeoff from Danang. (USAF)

A-6A of VMA(AW)-533 takes off from Nam Phong, an advanced airfield in Northern Thailand that was used by VMFA-115 and 232 as well as the A-6 squadron. (U.S. Marines)

(Above) A-4E of VMA-121 at Chu Lai, 1967. VMA-121 was one of five A-4 squadrons operating from that airfield. In addition to 121 they were VMA-211, 214, 223, and 311. The A-4 provided the bulk of quick reaction close air support missions for the Marines.

A-4E of VMA-311 at Ubon RTAB, 1968. It is loaded with 500lb high drag bombs with fuse extenders, which will insure their exploding above ground for maximum blast effect. (Al Piccirillo via Norm Taylor)

A-4E of VMA-211 "Wake Island Avengers" in the landing pattern. The larger hump back contained additional avionics. (Shinichi Ohtaki)

Though VMA-223s nickname was "Bulldogs", Sylvester provided some comic relief on the drop tank of this A-4. (Al Piccirillo via Norm Taylor)

One of the principle NVA anti-aircraft weapons was the Soviet-built 37mm. This example was displayed at Takhli RTAB after being presented to the 355th Wing by Thai Army personnel. It was one of the surviving pieces of a battery that had been attacked by F-105s of the wing after the shoot down of a FAC. It had been abandoned by the NVA gunners after the Thud attack. (Don Kutyna)

Marine KC-130 Tanker refuelling a RF-8 of VFP-63 off the USS Hancock over the Gulf of Tonkin. (U.S. Navy)

VMA-311 Skyhawks returning from a mission in I Corps of South Vietnam. (U.S. Marines)

VMA-311 Skyhawks on final approach. (Shinichi Ohtaki)

The first OV-10 Broncos had arrived at Danang in July, 1968. They belonged to VMO-2, which used them as FAC and light strike aricraft. (Norm Taylor)

The Thai Air Force operated the OV-10A from Don Muang RTAB, for reconnaissance missions. (U.S. Army)

(Above) T-28D of the 222nd Tactical Fighter Squadron, Royal Thia Air Force Tactical Air Command at Ubon RTAB. (Norm Taylor collection)

(Left) The Thai Air Force continued to operate the F-86 in the air defense role through 1970. (Don Kutyna)

(Below) Australian built B20 Canberras arrived at Phan Rang AB in April, 1967. They were under operational control of the 35th TFW, and flew up to 8 sorties per day in their first months of combat. This Canberra was photographed at Phu Cat AB by Norm Taylor.

Canberra of No. 2 Squadron, Royal Australian Air Force, returning to Phan Rang after a July, 1969 mission. As seen through the nose of the wingman's airplane. 70% of their missions were flown in the Mekong Delta area. (USAF)

(Above) RAAF munitions crewmen loading a 750lb bomb on the wingtip of one of the Canberras at Phan Rang in March, 1970. (USAF)

(Below) Australian Canberra enroute to a target in South Vietnam, March, 1970. No. 2 Squadron used the call sign "Magpie", and they were one of the most combat-effective units in South Vietnam, flying combat for over three years before losing their first airplane. (USAF)

(Above) C-130 of RAAF Number 37 Squadron at Vung Tau AB, RVN. The RAAF used the hercules for Strategic Airlift, moving men and material to and from Vietnam. (Andy Mutzig)

RAAF UH-1D Huey at Gia Ray, RVN. No. 9 Squadron operated the Huey in a variety of roles. (Dave Evans)

At 16, 17', 52" N, 106 m, 36', 59" E on the Ho Chi Minh Trail in Laos, a reconnaissance aircraft photographed a pair of camouflaged enemy trucks. Heavy cratering of the surrounding country side indicates how much pressure was kept on this vital supply route. (U.S Navy)

Camouflaged SAM missiles were struck by F-4s and A-4s in North Vietnam, despite heavy AAA fire from the battery (circled). (U.S. Navy)

An RA-5C Vigilante shot this picture of Kep Airfield in North Vietnam on 23 May, 1967. Fires are from burning Migs after an Air Wing Nine strike on the base. (U.S. Navy)

The Russians continued to supply the North Vietnamese with the majority of their war material needs, with the bulk of it arriving by sea. These Soviet ships are bound for the port of Haiphong. (U.S. Navy)

Coming Soon!
Lou Drendel's

AIR WAR
over
Southeast Asia

A Pictorial Record
Vol. 3 1971-1975